S0-AJI-464

S0-AJI-464

Centers
of Belief

The Grand Tour

Centers of Belief

Flavio Conti

Translated by Patrick Creagh

HBJ Press
a subsidiary of Harcourt Brace Jovanovich, Inc.
Boston

HBJ Press

President, Robert J. George

Publisher, Giles Kemp

Vice President, Richard S. Perkins, Jr.

Managing Director, Valerie S. Hopkins

Executive Editor, Marcia Heath

Series Editor, Carolyn Hall

Staff Editor, Chris Heath

Text Editors: John Bennet, Elizabeth S. Duvall, Judith E. Hanhisalo, Amanda Heller, Joyce Milton

Editorial Production: Karen E. English, Ann McGrath, Eric Brus, Betsie Brownell, Patricia Leal, Pamela George

Project Coordinator, Linda S. Behrens

Business Manager, Edward Koman

Marketing Director, John R. Whitman

Public Relations, Janet Schotta

Business Staff: Pamela Herlich, Joan Kenney

Architectural Consultant, Dennis J. DeWitt

Text Consultants: Janet Adams, Elizabeth R. DeWitt, Perween Hasan

Design Implementation, Designworks

Rizzoli Editore

Authors of the Italian Edition: Dr. Flavio Conti, P. Favole, G. Gattoni, G. M. Tabarelli

Idea and Realization, Harry C. Lindinger

General Supervisor, Luigi U. Re

Graphic Designer, Gerry Valsecchi

Coordinator, Vilma Maggioni

Photography Credits:
Aerofilms: pp. 58–59 / *Almasy:* p. 57, pp. 60–65 / *Borromeo:* pp. 121–129, p. 130 top left, p. 131 top left and bottom left, p. 132 / *Campeggi:* p. 73, p. 78 top / *Cauchetier:* p. 47, p. 49 bottom right / *Hassia:* p. 46 top and center, p. 49 bottom left / *Hassmann:* p. 9, pp. 12–17, p. 20 bottom, p. 32 / *Hutchinson:* p. 145 top / *Interfoto:* p. 41 / *Magnum-Burri:* p. 108 top, p. 110 top and bottom, p. 111, p. 112 top left and right, p. 113, p. 116 / *Meyer:* p. 130 top right, center left and right, bottom, p. 131 top right, center left and right, bottom right / *Pubbliaerfoto:* pp. 10–11, pp. 42–43, pp. 74–75 / *Radidi:* p. 66 top and bottom, pp. 137–144, p. 145 bottom, pp. 146–148 / *Ricciarini-Simion:* p. 50 top, p. 51 bottom left and right / *Scala:* pp. 18–19, p. 20 top, pp. 21–31, pp. 79–96 / *Scala-Bencini:* p. 153, p. 157 top left, p. 163 left, top right, bottom right, p. 158 bottom, pp. 160–161 / *Scala-Scarfiotti:* pp. 154–155, p. 156 left and right, p. 157 top right and bottom, p. 162 top and bottom, p. 158 top, p. 159 top, bottom left and right, p. 164 / *SEF:* p. 49 top / *Sheridan:* p. 44 top and left, p. 52, pp. 67–68 / *Stierlin:* p. 105, pp. 106–107, p. 108 bottom, p. 109 top and bottom, p. 112 bottom, pp. 114–115 / *Tomsich:* p. 45 top, center and bottom, p. 46 bottom, p. 48 top and bottom, p. 50 bottom, p. 51 top.

Library of Congress Catalog Card Number: 78-54066
ISBN: 0-15-003729-5

Printed in Hong Kong by Mandarin Publishers Limited

Editorial Supervisor, Gianfranco Malafarina

Research Organizer, Germano Facetti

U.S. Edition Coordinator, Natalie Danesi Murray

Contents

Preface

Centers of Belief

Every nation has its spiritual shrines, its centers of belief. In addition to their religious significance, they are centers of national heritage and tradition, focal points for the pride and dignity of a people. Like the fabled statue of Pallas Athena, which assured the safety of the city of Troy from the attacking Greeks, modern nations have their own palladiums. The Palladium of Troy had been given to Dardanus, the founder of the city, by Zeus, the ruler of the gods. It was believed that as long as the palladium remained within the walls of Troy, the city could not be taken.

The centers of belief described in this volume are places rather than sacred objects, but they are also symbols of national soul and experience. The genesis of such centers is often random and frequently unrecorded. But they represent the true reflection of the community that created them. These shrines also epitomize the art and culture of a nation, because the best talents and techniques—as well as greatest financial resources—were lavished upon them.

The Baptistery of San Giovanni in Florence has been a symbol of the city and its inhabitants for centuries. A beautifully proportioned Romanesque octagonal structure, it stands in the cathedral square. From the very first, it occupied a special place in the lives of the Floren-

tines, as it was the scene, twice a year, of mass baptisms—unbaptized persons being forbidden to enter a church proper.

Precise records of the original architect and the construction of the baptistery have been lost. It is known, however, that by the fourteenth century, the baptistery had become for Dante, a native Florentine, "il mio bel San Giovanni." Even so, the baptistery the poet admired was not so magnificent as it is today. During the Renaissance it was embellished with beautiful bands of inlaid marble and sculpted bronze doors by Lorenzo Ghiberti. It is not at all surprising that the baptistery was one of the first buildings restored by the Florentines after the terrible flood of 1966.

The city of Pisa, not far from Florence, possesses an equally splendid symbol of the faith of its people. Just inside the ancient city walls stands the cluster of monuments for which the city is famous throughout the world: the cathedral, the baptistery, the cemetery, and the Leaning Tower. The square is known as the Campo dei Miracoli, or Field of Miracles, and it is easy to see why. The white marble monuments stand on a cool, green lawn, a miracle of architectural harmony and balance. The motif of blind arcades and columns which adorns the quartet of buildings has been widely imitated. Today, the greatest attraction of the square is, of course, the

extraordinary Leaning Tower, which has come to symbolize Pisa the world over. It began to lean even while it was being constructed, and the topmost stories had to be slightly inclined back toward the vertical to prevent the collapse of the whole structure.

The mighty pyramids of Teotihuacán in central Mexico suffered a different hazard, that of neglect and oblivion. The huge thriving city of Teotihuacán was reduced to vast mounds and ruins long before the Toltecs and Aztecs adopted it as a place of pilgrimage. Its origins remain a mystery, and even its name was coined by subsequent peoples. Yet, it appears to have been a great religious center of Meso-America, closely linked with the worship of Quetzalcoatl, the divine Feathered Serpent, who brought art, civilization, and culture to the peoples of ancient Mexico. Today, this vast site near Mexico City, dominated by the massive pyramids of the Sun and the Moon, is gradually being restored by archaeologists, who continue to try to glean the intentions of its builders.

The Temple of the Tooth in Kandy, Sri Lanka, is a Buddhist shrine. The temple, begun during the seventeenth century, is a simple, red-roofed, white stucco building set among palm trees and overlooking a manmade lake. It is prized not because of its architecture, but because it houses a most sacred relic—the tooth of Buddha himself. The tooth lies on a golden lotus flower within several elaborately locked, jeweled caskets. It is rarely open to view, although it is carried with great ceremony, still within its locked caskets, in the yearly Esala Perahera festival, which attracts many thousands of both Buddhists and tourists. Kandy was the last capital of Ceylon before the British gained control of the whole island; and the Temple of the Tooth still stands as a symbol of Ceylonese resistance—a witness to the independence and pride of a people.

While the Temple of the Tooth is relatively simple, the architecture of Borobudur, a Buddhist temple in central Java, is conceptually and architecturally complex. Indeed, it has been called the most significant monument in the Southern Hemisphere. Built about A.D. 800, Borobudur takes the form of a symbolic temple mountain. It consists of many concentric terraces, which are meant to be climbed by the pilgrim in a symbolic journey from the damnation of the flesh and earthly pleasures toward enlightenment. In the topmost central domed shrine, an unfinished statue of a Buddha may be glimpsed. Perhaps this is the ultimate lesson of the temple, a sign that the whole truth can never be fully attained.

In contrast with the architectural complexity of Borobudur, the now-ruined Temple of Apollo at Delphi exemplifies Classical purity and simplicity. The straight, white marble columns of its temples and treasuries that looked out over the mountains formed one of the most sacred shrines of Greece. Pilgrims came from throughout the ancient Greek world to Delphi to worship Apollo, the sun god, and to consult the oracle. Faith and reason existed alongside each other in the Greek mind, and this duality is epitomized at Delphi. Pilgrims would pay dearly for advice from the oracle, despite the legendary ambiguity of her replies. But also engraved on the front of the Temple of Apollo was the fundamental precept "Know Thyself."

The tranquil little town of Mostar in the mountainous region of Herzegovina in Yugoslavia is a center of belief that is both political and religious. A Turkish garrison town during the sixteenth century, Mostar is noted for its fine old Karadžozbeg Mosque and remains a beacon of Islamic culture and religion in modern Yugoslavia. Moreover, this picturesque town, dominated by its old stone bridge arching over the Neretva River, also symbolizes the fervently independent spirit of the Slavic peoples. It was a center of the Slavic renaissance during Turkish occupation as well as of the Pan-Slavic movement during the Austrian administration at the end of the nineteenth century. It later became a stronghold of resistance against the fascists during World War II.

Mont-Saint-Michel rises out of the sea off the coast of northern France. According to legend, the archangel Michael commanded the bishop of the town of Avranches to build an abbey in his name on a rocky hill in the nearby forest of Scissy. Then early in the eighth century, a freak tide ripped out the forest, and the hill became an island.

Constructed on the steep slopes of this dramatically born island, the abbey is an architectural gem. One section of it is aptly named La Merveille (the Wonder). The abbey flourished for several centuries, attracting pilgrims from throughout Europe, until it was closed during the French Revolution. A few monks are still permitted to live there, but now the pilgrims visiting Mont-Saint-Michel are largely tourists. They come to wonder at both the faith and skill of those who built this monastery on a mountain amidst the surging tide.

Christian, Buddhist, Classical, Moslem, pre-Columbian—the sanctuaries in this volume are a testimony to the universality of religious faith. As these peoples believed, they built, passing on their faith, their visions, their passions, hopes, fears, and illusions. And at the same time, they created their palladiums, their links between the uncertainty of human destiny and the eternal serenity of the divine.

The Baptistery of Florence

Italy

Preceding page, the Piazza San Giovanni, known as the "hub of Florence." In the fifth century, when the original church and baptistery of Santa Reparata were built here, this site was on the northern outskirts of town, in the shadow of the old Roman walls. By the late Middle Ages, the whole area had become hopelessly congested, and the tombstones of a disused graveyard leaned against the walls of the original baptistery. Successive renovations cleared away some of the clutter and, in the thirteenth century, paved the present square, which is officially entitled the Piazza San Giovanni but universally called the Piazza del Duomo (Cathedral Square). Today, traffic fills most of the open space, but on holidays the square becomes the scene of fireworks, parades, and various traditional ceremonies.

Above left, the Cathedral of Santa Maria del Fiore, seen from the nearby hill of San Miniato. Brunelleschi's great dome, the largest dome constructed in Italy since the Roman Pantheon, is visible from fifteen miles away. A street in the neighboring village of Pistoia, the Via dell'Apparenzia, was named to mark the spot where the dome first comes into view.

The octagonal shape of the Baptistery of San Giovanni (left, below left, and facing page) was echoed in the design for the cathedral dome. San Giovanni's interior was originally arranged around a baptismal font designed to accommodate mass infant baptisms, which were held two times a year in accordance with a custom that had been observed in this part of Italy since the early Christian era. Because the unbaptized were not permitted to enter a church proper, the sacrament was always performed in a separate building. The ornamental "lantern" on the baptistery roof (below) was added in about 1174. Its shape recalls a miniature Classical temple.

The Cathedral of Santa Maria del Fiore was begun in 1296, but by the mid-1400s, Florence had been seized by the spirit of the Renaissance. Later generations considered the cathedral's half-finished Gothic façade so outdated that it was eventually torn off in anticipation of a Baroque replacement, which was never actually erected. Ironically, when the façade was finally replaced during the nineteenth century, taste had come full circle and the design chosen (left) was Neo-Gothic.

Decorative painting and sculpture from the fifteenth century may still be seen above the side doors of the cathedral. The most celebrated of these doors is the Porta della Mandorla on the north side of the cathedral. The gable relief crowning this entrance (below far left) is the work of Donatello's contemporary, Nanni d'Antonio di Banco. Its subject is the Assumption of the Virgin, but it was di Banco's use of the mandorla, or almond, motif which gave the door its name. Below left, a nineteenth-century gable relief above one of the side doors.

Above right, the east and north tribunes of the fourteenth-century apse. Below near right, the Porta della Mandorla, showing the lunette mosaic of the Annunciation by Domenico and Davide Ghirlandajo (1491). The small figures, known as the prophets, on either side of the door frame are variously attributed to Nanni di Banco or Donatello. Most of the Renaissance sculpture by Donatello, Luca della Robbia, and others, which once adorned other parts of the cathedral and the nearby bell tower, has been removed to a museum to protect it from the effects of pollution. Center far right, a nineteenth-century tympanum above the right-hand door of the façade. Below far right, a niche statuary just below the rose window in the nineteenth-century façade.

Giotto's famous campanile, or bell tower, over 260 feet in height, is universally considered the architectural gem of Florence. Although Giotto died two years after construction on the tower began in 1334, his plans were for the most part honored by later architects, resulting in a unity of form and decoration which the rest of the cathedral complex does not quite achieve. The campanile's graceful façade (facing page and right) is composed of inlaid Tuscan marble: the white from Carrara, the green from Prato, and the red from the Maremma region. The tower, which is open to the public, affords a panoramic view of Florence and some unusual vantage points for studying the cathedral (above and below).

Renaissance Florentines believed that the Baptistery of San Giovanni was an actual Roman building whose survival symbolized the city's unique Classical heritage. The precise age of San Giovanni cannot be documented, but its architectural style is Romanesque rather than Roman, and it was probably constructed in the eleventh century.

Above and above left, two views of the small apse of San Giovanni, popularly known as "la scarsella" (the purse), which was built in 1202 to make room for an altar within.

Another later addition to the baptistery is the attic, or third story (left and above right), whose ornamentation reveals the increasing influence of Classicism.

Right, two marble statues by the sixteenth-century sculptor Andrea Sansovino, representing the Baptism of Christ. The angel who watches over the scene was created in the eighteenth century and is thus, by Florentine standards, a modern work.

To Dante, the baptistery was "il mio bel San Giovanni," *the symbol of the city he longed for throughout two decades of political exile. For Florentines of the next century, it was a focus of civic pride, inspiring their determination to create a "new Athens" on the banks of the Arno. Every generation, it seems, looks at the baptistery with new eyes. Present-day visitors usually come to admire the building's famous masterpieces, but the site also has many purely religious associations. Beside the baptistery stands the Pillar of St. Zenobius (above), erected in 1384 to commemorate an early Christian miracle. It is said that in A.D. 433, when the saint's bones were being moved to the Church of Santa Reparata, the holy procession was caught in a sudden storm and took shelter under a withered elm tree, which suddenly sprouted leaves to protect the relics from the rain.*

Left, detail of the attic of San Giovanni.

A close examination of the baptistery's façade (facing page) shows that its apparent regularity is really an illusion. Subtle changes in the detail and proportion, such as widening and raising the arches over the doors, were built into the design to avoid monotony.

The Porta del Paradiso (facing page) was so named by Michelangelo, who declared it worthy to be the door to heaven itself. This treasure was damaged in the flood of 1966. The panels that were dislodged have been perfectly restored.

The door's gilded bronze reliefs, cast by Lorenzo Ghiberti between 1425 and 1452, are far more realistic in composition and detail than the sculptor's previous work and show his evolution toward a true Renaissance sensibility. Each of the ten panels represents an episode from the Old Testament. This page, clockwise from top to left: the story of Jacob and Esau, the patriarch Abraham, a decorative figure from the right doorjamb, a self-portrait of the artist, and the story of Joseph.

Ghiberti's first set of baptistery doors (above far left) was commissioned as the result of an open competition announced in 1401. The judges preferred Ghiberti's designs to a more modern but technically less exacting plan submitted by Filippo Brunelleschi, the future architect of the cathedral dome. A detail from the reliefs (far left) depicts the Adoration of the Magi.

The Porta del Paradiso (left) swings open to reveal the interior of the baptistery. An imposing figure of Christ in Judgment dominates the mosaic decorations of the vault. Traced on the pavement below is the outline of the baptismal font, which was removed during the sixteenth century.

Above, the interior of "la scarsella," a rectangular apse opening off the west wall of the building. Wooden choir stalls which originally screened it from view were removed in 1577. A later Baroque altar has also been replaced.

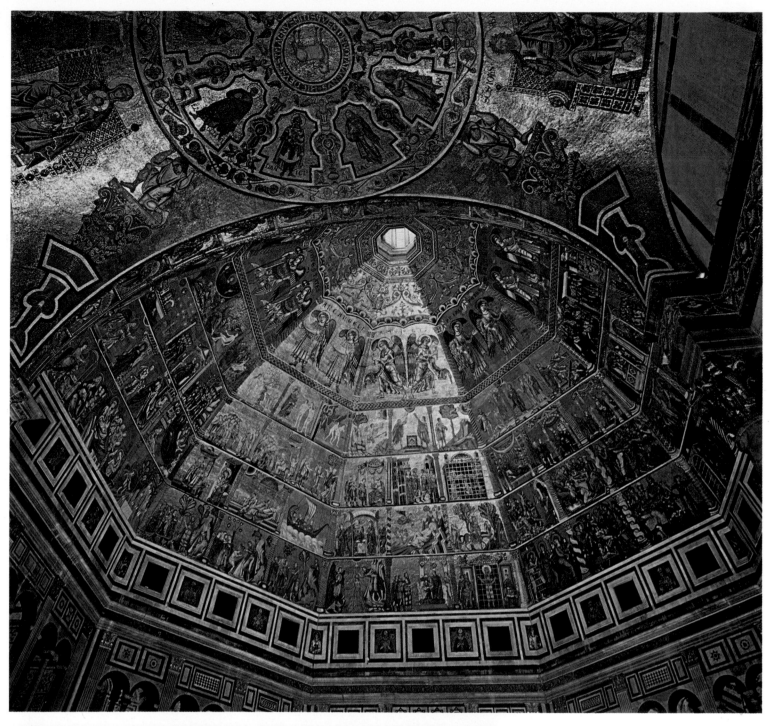

Inside the baptistery (above far left) are antique Oriental granite Corinthian columns supporting an arcade. They are said to have been salvaged from Roman ruins. The site of the baptistery is known to have been continuously occupied since the first century A.D. The ravaged features of Mary Magdalene (center left) are a late example of the work of Donatello. Another Donatello masterpiece, produced thirty years earlier, is the tomb of Baldasare Coscia (far left). Coscia held office as Pope John XXIII but was later declared an illegally elected antipope. The name John went unused by subsequent popes until the twentieth century, when Cardinal Roncalli became the legitimate Pope John XXIII.

Above and left, the gilded mosaics, which were Florence's answer to the widely acclaimed mosaic cycle in St. Mark's Church in Venice.

The baptistery mosaics are as much a monument to Florence's wealth as its piety. Begun in the thirteenth century and finished about 1330, they were sponsored by the Calimala—the wool merchants' guild. Textile manufacturing, along with banking, was the basis of the city's economic and cultural revival. Most of the actual work on the mosaics was done by Venetian craftsmen, but native artists, including Giotto's teacher, Cimabue, probably provided some of the original designs. Although the style of the mosaics recalls Byzantium, their subject was one which preoccupied the plague-ridden world of the late Middle Ages—the Last Judgment. Below, one of the largest panels, depicting sinners being delivered into the jaws of hell. Left and right, details of the narrative panels that line the cupola. The top rows depict scenes from the life of Christ; the bottom ones dramatize the martyrdom of John the Baptist. The dance of Salome is shown at far right.

SCS·IOHS· BA·TIST·

Unlike the realistic tableaux of the Porta del Paradiso, the mosaics of the baptistery depend heavily on conventional symbolic depictions. Clockwise from top left, further details of the mosaic cycle: Christ and two Apostles on the Sea of Galilee, the Nativity, the Adoration of the Magi, a decorative detail and inscription, Joseph imprisoned in Egypt, Joseph's reunion with his father, John the Baptist, the kiss of Judas, and the Virgin Mary.

Following page, the campanile and the Cathedral of Santa Maria del Fiore with its magnificent Brunelleschi dome. The gallery at the base of the dome was begun in 1508. Michelangelo derisively called it the "cricket cage," and it remains unfinished to this day.

The Baptistery of Florence Italy

Dante called it *"il mio bel San Giovanni"* (my beautiful San Giovanni). But his nostalgic tribute to the Baptistery of San Giovanni in Florence, the place of his own baptism, was tinged with bitterness, for it was written while the poet was in exile. He had been driven from his native city after entering, passionately but inexpertly, into the factional politics that dominated Florentine life. The author of the *Divine Comedy* loved the elegance of Florence, epitomized for him in the Baptistery of San Giovanni, but he was critical of the ambitious and quarrelsome temper of its citizens. He was, as he said, a Florentine by birth, but not by behavior.

Dante's praise of the *"bel San Giovanni"* still echoes through the baptistery, repeated by tour guides to visitors who honor the poet's name but often know little of his life or work. Many do not realize that the triumphs of Renaissance art in Florence did not even exist when Dante was banished from the city in 1302. The Florence he remembered so fondly was a medieval one. The Uffizi Palace and its masterpieces by Botticelli, Filippo Lippi, and Paolo Uccello had not yet been dreamed of. The Cathedral of Santa Maria del Fiore, which stands next to the baptistery, was in the earliest stages of construction. The painter Giotto was still a young man and had not yet designed his campanile (bell tower), which now stands in the cathedral square. And Lorenzo Ghiberti, the designer of the sculpted doors which today are the crowning glory of the baptistery, had not even been born.

In the century following Dante's exile, Florence was a city that depended on the ingenuity and resourcefulness of its inhabitants for its prosperity. And its growing businesses and rich outlying farm lands had to be defended against powerful neighbors that threatened the city on all sides and controlled its access to the sea and to Rome.

In the second half of the 1300s, the chief rival of Florence was Milan. The ruler of Milan, Duke Gian Galeazzo Visconti, was campaigning to bring most of Italy under his control; and Florence, with its endless internal political struggles, might have been expected to collapse in the face of this challenge. Yet exactly the opposite occurred, for the Visconti threat disappeared quite suddenly and unexpectedly with the death of the duke of Milan in 1402. But even before, in those tumultuous times, the Florentines had aspired to make their city a center of art and philosophy. Money was raised through taxes and private donations for civic improvements worthy of a "new Athens." And it was these improvements that signaled the emergence of the Renaissance style.

One stage of the program of improvements was the installation of a new set of doors for the Baptistery of San Giovanni, and in 1401, the city announced an open competition for the commission. The winner was Lorenzo Ghiberti. Ghiberti cast a beautiful set of bronze doors with high relief panels depicting scenes from the life and Passion of Christ. His work won universal admiration, and when the doors were completed some twenty-five years later, he was immediately asked to begin a second set. These, decorated with tableaux based on the Old Testament, were even more stunning. Michelangelo pronounced them worthy to be the gateway to paradise itself, and ever since, the Porta del Paradiso has been the baptistery's acknowledged masterpiece. The doors were given the place of honor facing the cathedral

Right, scene of Florence in a miniature from the Biadaiola. *Shields bearing the lily, the emblem of the city, decorate the tower. To the right is the octagonal form of the Baptistery of San Giovanni.*

square, replacing an earlier set cast by Andrea Pisano in 1336, which was moved to the less important south entrance.

Although Ghiberti was essentially part of the tradition of medieval craftsmanship, his famous relief sculptures were the product of a sensibility in transition, poised between the Gothic and the Renaissance views of the world. And even as Ghiberti was beginning to cast the first of his doors, the runner-up in the competition for their design was embarking on a new career which would complete that transition.

This runner-up was a young goldsmith named Filippo Brunelleschi, who was so disappointed by his defeat that he decided to give up metalwork and study architecture in Rome. With a friend named Donatello—another finalist in the competition, who was later to become famous as a sculptor—Brunelleschi spent his time sketching ancient ruins in Rome, where he developed a love for architecture. Both Brunelleschi and Donatello were true Renaissance artists. They were as much at home in the realm of ideas as in the atelier of the craftsman. In fact, it was Brunelleschi who perfected the system of linear perspective which was to revolutionize the art of painting.

The Baptistery of San Giovanni itself belongs not to the Renaissance but to the Middle Ages. Built in the mid-eleventh century, it exemplifies the serene Tuscan Romanesque style. The building is an octagon, which was originally laid out around a central baptismal font. About halfway up the exterior is a visual witticism: a two-dimensional suggestion of a blind arcade. The tops of the arcade's pilasters just barely touch the bottoms of its arches at their corners, thus emphasizing their nonstructural decorative character.

Throughout its history, the baptistery exerted an influence which far surpassed either its architectural or functional importance. Although it is a relatively small building, it held a special place in the religious life of the city. Twice annually it was the scene of mass infant baptisms. An old Christian tradition, which forbade unbaptized persons from entering the church

Above, detail from the fresco La Madonna della Misericordia *in the loggia of the Bigallo Palace in Florence, showing a panorama of the city in the fourteenth century. Below, Dante Alighieri, in a fresco by Domenico di Michelino in the Cathedral of Santa Maria del Fiore.*

proper, necessitated a separate building for baptisms.

The font was a pool large enough for the immersion of infants, which the baptismal ritual required. There were also a number of sunken niches around the font where the priests stood during the ceremony. In the *Divine Comedy,* Dante relates a story—which may or may not be true—of how, on one occasion, when he was attending a baptism, a child tripped and fell into one of these pits. The poet immediately went to the child's rescue, damaging the cover of the niche in the process. He thus earned at one and the same time the gratitude of the parents of the child and the reputation of a sacrilegious vandal—a reputation that dogged him throughout his life.

By the end of the fourteenth century, the baptistery had become emblematic of artistic as well as religious sentiments. The Florentines of that era were convinced that the building dated back to Classical times. Even Brunelleschi, who had seen enough of Roman ruins to be an expert on the subject, apparently accepted this notion. For Brunelleschi and his contemporaries, the Baptistery of San Giovanni was a source of artistic inspiration, just as it had been a spiritual one for Dante.

This belief in the baptistery's antiquity, which persisted into modern times, had some basis in fact. The remains of previous Christian and Roman buildings appear to lie under the baptistery floor, and a few elements in the present construction may survive from its early Christian predecessor. The Florentines identified strongly with the spirit of the Roman republic, but the underlying Roman edifice, once tentatively identified as the "Praetorium" but most probably a bakery, dates only from the first century A.D. when Florence was at best a provincial imperial settlement.

Most historians agree that the original baptistery on the present site was built in the early fifth century. At that time, the square, where the baptistery and the cathedral stand, was not in the center of the city. The square was merely an empty space on the outskirts of town, adjacent to the old Roman walls. This location was chosen for a parish church that would commemorate the salvation of Florence from the Visigoths. According to tradition, the siege of the Goths was repulsed on October 8, 405, by the timely arrival of Roman legions under the imperial general Stilicho. Both the new church and its baptistery were named in honor of Santa Reparata, a Syrian martyr whose feast day happened to coincide with the date of the battle.

Like Saint John the Baptist, the city's official patron saint, Santa Reparata was not a Florentine and had no historical association with the city. This circumstance, though not uncommon, eventually became a source of irritation to the proud Florentines. They therefore dispatched a committee to a convent near Teano in southern Italy to purchase Santa Reparata's relics. The envoys returned triumphant with the saint's arm and right hand, purchased for their weight in gold, and these acquisitions were installed in the church with great ceremony. There they remained despite the discovery a few years later that the convent had tricked the Florentines, foisting off plaster casts in

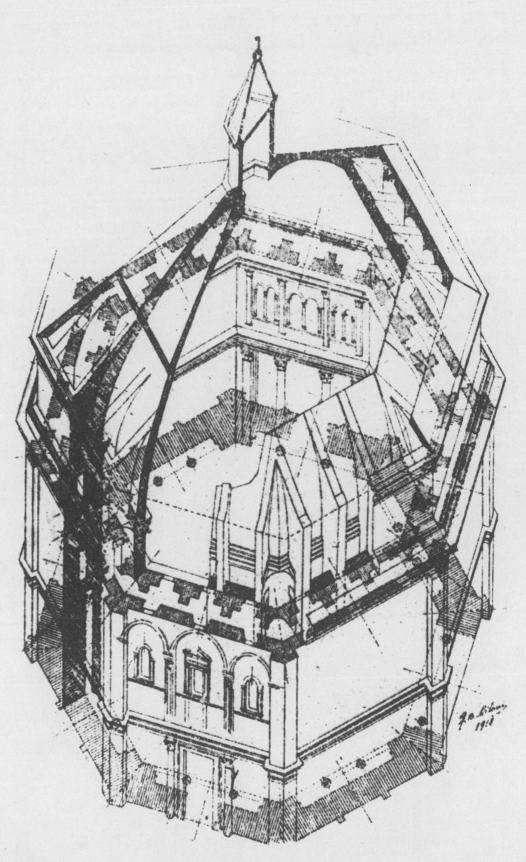

An axonometric drawing (above right) details the interior structure of the baptistery dome.

place of the true relics. This deception, so damaging to the Florentines' reputation as shrewd businessmen, was kept quiet, and for years the faithful were allowed to pay homage to the spurious bones.

In the early part of the Middle Ages, Florence had survived a number of challenges to its existence. During one period of plague and famine, the population was reduced to a mere few hundred inhabitants, and packs of wild dogs roamed the nearly deserted streets. By the year 1057, however, the city was again thriving and had become for a time the official seat of the marchioness of Tuscany within the Holy Roman Empire. Santa Reparata, which by now stood near the center of the expanding city, shared the new prosperity. It was named the bishop's own church, the official cathedral of Florence.

At this time, the old baptistery was replaced by the present Romanesque structure dedicated to Saint John the Baptist. The exact dates and details of this building project have been lost, but it is known that a consecration ceremony was held in 1059, and until 1128, the new baptistery served as the cathedral proper while the Church of Santa Reparata was undergoing reconstruction. San Giovanni itself was constantly being improved and altered, so much so that the later confusion about its true age is hardly surprising. In the twelfth century, the roof was raised by the addition of a new vault. In 1174, the vault was topped off by an ornamental

Much research—and some wild speculation—has been undertaken in an attempt to determine the exact date of the baptistery. Above, two designs for the façade. These are one researcher's suggestions of how the building would have looked, had it been built in the thirteenth century with the pointed arches used by Arnolfo di Cambio (left) or in the Romanesque period (right)—as in fact it was. These designs, made in the early twentieth century, were intended to show that the baptistery was definitely built before the eleventh century.

Below far left, a Renaissance plan of the original arrangement of the baptistery.

Center, a nineteenth-century composite plan showing a hypothetical reconstruction of the original arrangement of the baptistery, with other subsequent arrangements superimposed.

Below, a cross section of the baptistery. The upper part of the diagram shows the gallery level, the lower part the roof supports.

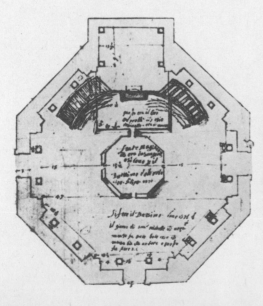

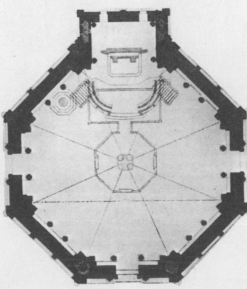

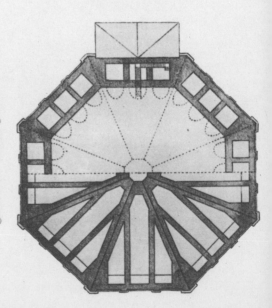

"lantern" that looks like a small colonnaded temple and echoes the shape of the whole building. A small apse that would house the altar more appropriately was added to the building's western side in 1202. It quickly acquired the nickname "*la scarsella*" because it reminded local wags of the small purses that dangled from the belts of fashionable Florentines.

The interior of the baptistery was also transformed, most notably by the impressive mosaics lining the vaults. These were begun in the first half of the thirteenth century and finally completed in the 1330s. The mosaics were largely the work of Venetian artists, hired by the wool merchants guild which did not want the churches of Florence to be inferior to St. Mark's in Venice. Art historians sometimes argue that these masterpieces in the Byzantine style do not quite fit in with the rest of the baptistery, which otherwise embodies the evolution of native Tuscan art. Nevertheless, they are among San Giovanni's most admired works.

The years between 1300 and 1400 constituted a transitional period for Italian art. In a sense, the Baptistery of San Giovanni, like all of Florence, became a workshop for the emerging style. This new outlook was evident in Ghiberti's work on the baptistery doors over several decades. It was even more readily apparent in the work on the new cathedral, officially known as Santa Maria del Fiore. In 1296, the Sienese architect Arnolfo di Cambio was asked to design a church "such that the industry and power of man could not invent anything greater or more beautiful." He accordingly drew up plans for an immense Italian Gothic cathedral, and work began promptly under the supervision of a public committee known as the Opera del Duomo. After di Cambio died in 1302, his plans were subjected to a number of revisions by his successors.

Some of the designers who followed di Cambio were not architects at all but painters. Their skills may not have been ideally suited to the task of building a cathedral, but the Opera del Duomo recognized in these men the true creative talents of the era. The most important of the painter-architects was Giotto, who, in 1334, was asked to design a campanile. Giotto envisioned a tall, slender tower topped by a spire that would balance the grandeur of the cathedral and unify the architectural elements of the square. Like many modifications suggested for the cathedral itself, these plans were never quite completed. Today, the bell tower stands approximately 260 feet tall, lacking the spire which would have added another 100 feet to its height. When Giotto died in 1336, work on the tower had barely begun. Except for the spire, his conception was faithfully carried out by later artists, among them Andrea Pisano, who also cast the first of the three sets of baptistery doors.

After 1339, work on the cathedral was interrupted by a series of calamities, including the threat of conquest by the Viscontis of Milan. Not until the end of the century did the Florentines find the enthusiasm and the funds to continue. Ghiberti's commission for the baptistery doors was only the first of the renewed efforts. More important, it now seemed that the Cathedral of Santa Maria del Fiore could at last be finished. But one obstacle remained, which money could not remove.

All the architects on the cathedral project had assumed that the design would be completed by a suitably grand dome, but none of them knew how to build such a structure. Architects of the Middle Ages were not especially interested in domes. Although there were a number of Byzan-

Below, a mid-nineteenth century hypothesis (which has since been rejected) of how the apse of the baptistery may have looked before its demolition in 1576. The design is based upon other churches which are contemporary with the baptistery.

Above, the baptistery vault, showing the overall plan of the mosaic cycle. The panels nearest Christ depict the Judgment Day; others narrate Bible stories.

tine domes, no dome of comparable dimensions had been built in Italy since the Roman Pantheon, completed in the second century A.D. Moreover, the partial collapse of the dome of the church of Hagia Sophia in Constantinople in 1347 was a reminder that building domed structures was a risky undertaking. The confidence of the Opera del Duomo could not have been enhanced by the knowledge that the supplementary buttresses which had failed to hold Hagia Sophia together were the work of Italians.

In 1418, the Opera del Duomo announced an open competition for a design for the dome. One entry, that of Filippo Brunelleschi, was clearly more daring than all the rest. The former goldsmith's proposal called for a pointed vault which would span 132 feet entirely without the aid of buttresses or other external supports. Brunelleschi also assured the Opera del Duomo that the vault could be raised without scaffolding—a major consideration, since building wooden scaffolds to the required height would have been prohibitively expensive and, quite probably, physically impossible.

Brunelleschi's unusual plan was based on a double-shelled dome. The distance between the two domes allowed him to place unseen vertical ribs—essentially Gothic—along the joints between the sides of his octagonal shell and to encircle the dome with wooden, reinforcing chains, bound together with iron connectors. To the Classical mind, these chains were superior to the massive buttresses they supplanted, since they were completely hidden from view.

Although Brunelleschi is credited with having "invented" the Renaissance with his aesthetic innovations, his structural advances were often too complicated for his contemporaries to grasp, let alone endorse. The Opera del Duomo initially doubted whether Brunelleschi could build a dome that lacked both internal supports and external buttresses. One of the chief skeptics was Brunelleschi's old rival Lorenzo Ghiberti. To convince the Opera that his dome would be structurally sound, Brunelleschi built a large-scale model on the banks of the Arno. He finally won the commission. But Ghiberti, who was by then an official consultant to the Opera, continued to criticize the plans, impeding progress at every turn. Brunelleschi eventually resorted to a trick worthy of farce. Feigning illness, he retired to his home and asked that the work be put under Ghiberti's supervision. Left to himself, the sculptor-craftsman Ghiberti quickly made a mess of the job and retreated in confusion to the project he should have been concentrating on all along—the baptistery doors. Brunelleschi then graciously consented to return. His dome was completed in 1436 and became an immediate sensation, inspiring countless imitations throughout Europe.

The architecture of Brunelleschi and the sculpture of his friend Donatello—whose wooden statue of Mary Magdalene, once deemed shockingly realistic, stands in the Baptistery of San Giovanni—were only the first stirrings of an artistic movement that would make Florence the cultural capital of the Western world for two centuries. Their era largely completed the development of the baptistery and its immediate architectural environment. In years to come, the changes that were made were not always for the better. In 1576, for example, an architect with the ill-deserved name of Buontalenti (good talents) removed from the baptistery a baptismal font which dated from Dante's time. He also tore out irreplaceable carved wooden choir stalls to make the interior "more convenient" for the baptism of the latest Medici heir.

The original Gothic façade of Santa Maria del Fiore fared even worse. To the sixteenth-century Florentines, it seemed hopelessly old-fashioned, and it was never completed. The façade was torn off in anticipation of a Baroque façade, which was never actually realized. Instead, there were a series of temporary plaster concoctions and scores of unrealized reconstruction plans submitted by lesser architects. Finally, in the late nineteenth century, taste having come full circle, the façade was redone in a popular contemporary style—Neo-Gothic.

Changing standards of taste were not, however, the most formidable menace. The ultimate assault on the baptistery and cathedral was the great flood of 1966, which devastated the city of Florence and

Above right, detail of the baptistery's second-story arcade.

A photograph (right) taken in 1887 shows work in progress on reconstruction of the cathedral façade.

buried some of its most precious treasures under tons of mud. The oily waters of the Arno reached the baptistery itself, damaging the doors cast by Andrea Pisano and tearing panels from the Porta del Paradiso. Fortunately, all the original relief work on the doors was recovered, save one lion's head from the Pisano doors. This has been recast, however, from another similar figure. Donatello's wooden statue of Mary Magdalene, which was discolored when the flood waters swept through the interior of the baptistery, also proved restorable. Elsewhere in Florence, the night of November 4, 1966, marked the destruction of libraries and paintings, homes and industries. But the city did recover. Its inhabitants began the work of rebuilding with typical Florentine determination, first attacking the muck with their bare hands, and later rescuing much of their artistic heritage with the aid of a massive international effort.

The city immediately resumed its annual civic festival. This celebration dates back to the Middle Ages and was no doubt witnessed by Dante himself. Every Easter Sunday, Florentines gather in the cathedral square to join in an unusual rite, the *Scoppio del Carro,* or Exploding of the Cart. This ceremonial rekindling of sacred flames has been traditional since the time of the Crusades, when a soldier of fortune returned from Jerusalem bearing fragments of the Holy Sepulcher. These fragments were struck together like flints to produce a flame which was then distributed to the faithful.

Today, the "cart," four stories high, and gilded, paneled, tassled, and topped with a crown, stops before the cathedral. From the high altar, a mechanical dove on a wire swoops through the open door and strikes the cart which is laden with fireworks. The cart then bursts into flames before the appreciative crowd and the alert fire brigade. The descendants of the soldier have historically had the honor of setting up the cart.

It is said that if the dove slides down the wire easily, lighting the firecrackers without human intervention, the city will be blessed with good fortune in the coming year. On the other hand, if it fails, hard times will prevail. This superstition appeals to the Florentine sense of the dramatic. However, the "new Athens" of the Renaissance was built not on luck but on a solid foundation of civic commitment and individual enterprise, uniting financial resources, technological innovation, and artistic talents in the service of a single ideal.

Below, Florence in about 1490. At this time, the city was at the height of its wealth and power under one of its greatest rulers, Lorenzo the Magnificent.

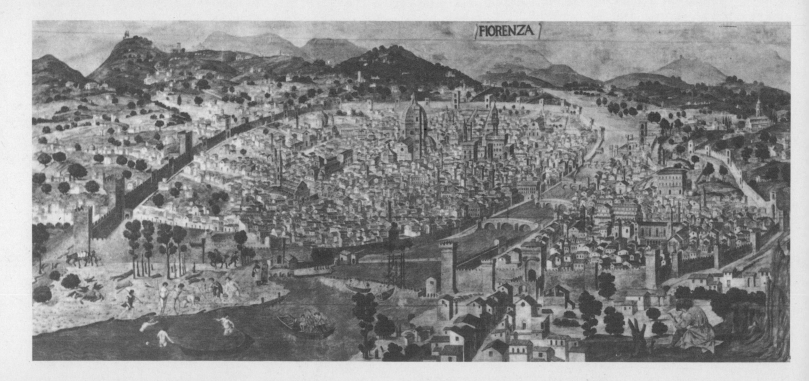

The Sanctuary
at Delphi

Greece

Preceding page, the excavations at Delphi, showing the theater, the Temple of Apollo in the center, and below it the reconstructed Treasury, or storehouse, of the Athenians. Systematic excavations of the site were begun in the nineteenth century by the French Archaeological School at Athens. The Sacred Way, lined with the ruins of monuments from all the Greek city-states and colonies, zigzags up to the temple.

Above and far right center, the columns of the Temple of Apollo. The Greeks built their columns as a series of drums which were joined in the center by metal dowels and finished so finely that the joints were imperceptible.

Right, the remains of the Temple of Apollo, which was built with funds contributed by every Greek city-state as well as by foreigners, such as the pharaoh of Egypt.

Above far right, the theater, whose 33 tiers of limestone seats held about 5,000 spectators. Below far right, the reconstructed ruins of the altar of the Temple of Apollo.

Left, the ancient caverns inhabited by the sibyls, peasant women who supposedly possessed powers of prophecy. In a divine frenzy, they would foretell the future of those who consulted them. The caves were later used as tombs.

Center, the path in the Castalian Gorge leading to the sanctuary. In ancient times, water from the celebrated spring was used by suppliants for ritual purification before they ascended to the sacred area of the sanctuary.

Below left, all that remains of the eight-columned stoa, or portico, built by the Athenians in the early fifth century B.C. to display the booty taken from the ships of the Persian King Xerxes. It stands before the retaining wall of polygonal stones that served to support the terrace of the Temple of Apollo.

Facing page, the tholos, or round temple, built around 390 B.C. in the sanctuary of Athena Pronaia. Theodoros of Phocaea, its architect, adapted the forms of Greek temple architecture to this round shape. Originally, there was an outer colonnade of twenty Doric columns surrounding a cylindrical cella (central room) within which was another colonnade of ten Corinthian columns. A conical roof covered the cella and the outer colonnade. The function of the building is uncertain, but it is generally thought to have been used for religious or funerary purposes.

Above left, the Treasury of the Athenians, erected in 490 B.C. after the Battle of Marathon. Built of Parian marble, it takes the form of two columns standing between extended walls which enclose the porch. This treasury represents the ultimate achievement of the archaic Doric style: harmony and purity of lines and volumes, balance between the various forms of the order, freedom from the heaviness of the earlier Archaic period without the geometric rigidity of the later Classical era. The treasury was rebuilt by the French in 1904, using as much of the original marble as possible.

Left, the remains of an Ionic column from the Treasury of the Corinthians. Above right, the Sacred Way which leads up to the Temple of Apollo. In antiquity it was lined with treasuries, statues, thank-offerings, and memorials of all the Greek cities. Right, a white marble stele, or upright stone, which displays a bull in bas-relief. Far right, inscriptions on the polygonal wall supporting the Temple of Apollo which date from the third century B.C. The walls were used as a public forum for comments and opinions. Over 700 inscriptions survive, primarily dealing with the emancipation of slaves.

Above, a section of a bas-relief frieze from the Treasury of the Siphnians, depicting scenes from the Trojan War. Here the Greek hero Menelaus and his son are fighting for the body of their comrade Patroclus against the Trojans Hector and Aeneas. The frieze was originally painted in bright colors, traces of which can be seen in this fragment.

Right, the famous Charioteer of Delphi, a life-size bronze statue cast about 470 B.C. The statue was part of a chariot group dedicated by Poly-zalus of Syracuse to the Temple of Apollo in the fifth century B.C.

Above far right, detail of the north frieze of the Siphnian Treasury, depicting a battle between gods and giants. One of the lions harnessed to the chariot of the goddess Cybele is attacking a giant as he tries to escape.

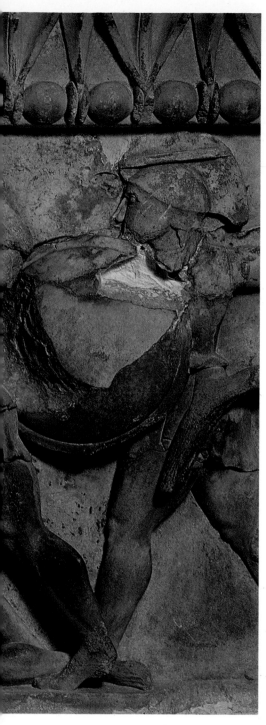

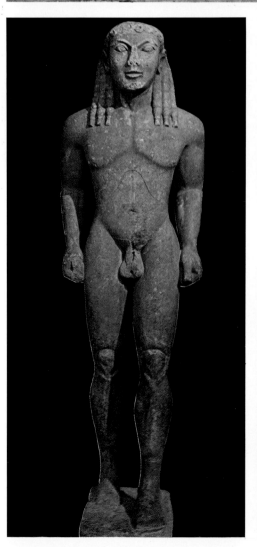

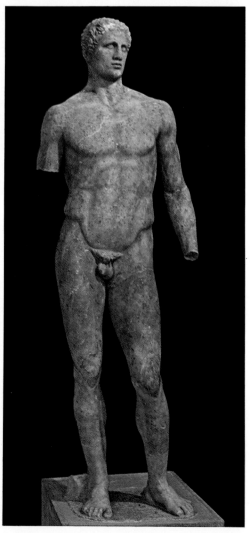

Right, one of a pair of statues of the twins Kleobis and Byton by Polymedes, executed in the early Archaic style of around 600 B.C. The young man, in his prime, is helping to pull his mother's chariot to the temple. Far right, a marble copy of a later, less stylized bronze statue of an athlete named Agias by Lysippus. The original dates from about 340 B.C. Agias is praised as the first Thessalian to win the pancratium (a contest that involves both wrestling and boxing) at the Olympiad.

Following page, the theater at the sanctuary of Delphi. Beyond, the remains of the Temple of Apollo can be seen against the Phaedriades, or "shining cliffs."

The Sanctuary at Delphi Greece

Today, the steep mountain side between towering crags is strewn with ruins. On clear days, the stones of Delphi shine in the intense sunlight, and the nearby sea, though not actually visible, makes itself felt in the dazzling brightness of the sky.

Delphi was highly revered by the early Greeks. In the most ancient times, they worshiped Gaea, the goddess of the earth, at this shrine. In the Classical era, when the gods of the sky gained ascendancy over those of the earth, the sun god Apollo was venerated at Delphi and assumed the role of protector of the sacred shrine.

Delphi was spiritually, although not geographically, the center of the Greek world. It was said that Zeus, father and ruler of the gods, one day asked himself which point on the earth's surface was its

center. To find out, he released two of his sacred eagles at the same moment, one from the easternmost point of the world and the other from the west, commanding them to fly until they met. They eventually alighted at Delphi where a stone, called the *omphalos,* or navel, was placed to mark the "navel of the world." Around it was built a sanctuary to which Greeks came from all the city-states of mainland Greece, the Aegean Islands, Asia Minor, and even the Greek colonies in southern Italy and Sicily.

The most picturesque approach to Delphi is through the Gulf of Corinth. The traveler sailing down the Balkan coast of the Adriatic passes a number of islands: first Corfu, then big Cephalonia, and little Ithaca, the homeland of Odysseus. Opposite these islands is the opening to a long, narrow channel. This is the Gulf of Corinth that divides the northern shore of the Peloponnese from the mainland of Greece. Not far from here, in 31 B.C., the ships of Octavian defeated those of Mark Antony at the Battle of Actium, and Octavian became Augustus, the first Roman emperor.

About halfway along the gulf on the northern shore, there is a small bay and a port called Itéa, or Cirrha, as it was known

in ancient times. Cirrha was the harbor used by the pilgrims who arrived at Delphi from every part of the Greek world. It lies at the end of the fertile valley of the Pleistos which rises steeply toward the slopes of Mount Parnassus, the mountain sacred to the wine god Dionysus.

The sides of Mount Parnassus, the second highest mountain in Greece, form three great cliffs called the Phaedriades, or "shining cliffs." In a space between these barren rocks—where a cool stream called the Castalian Fountain, or Spring of the Muses, once flowed—the Greeks constructed their shrine.

The sanctuary of Delphi is so ancient that it has been sacred to many gods during the development of Hellenic civilization. We know very little about the first inhabitants of Greece, who were called Pelasgians, or sea people, by the later Classical Greeks. But we do know that they worshiped Gaea, the goddess of the earth, at Delphi, along with her daughter Themis, goddess of law and justice.

Then men began to come across the sea from Crete. They were merchants and sailors, who worshiped a sea god, Poseidon. Moisture, springs, and streams which give life to the earth were the province of Poseidon, who was also Gaea's lover. Without too much difficulty, the cults of

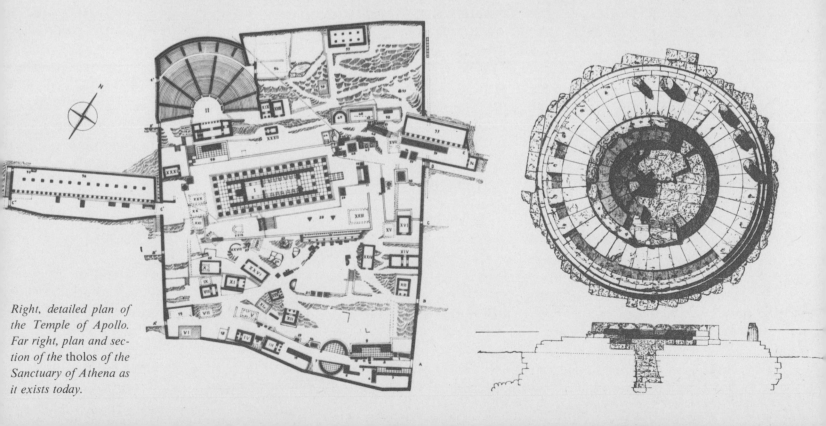

Right, detailed plan of the Temple of Apollo. Far right, plan and section of the tholos *of the Sanctuary of Athena as it exists today.*

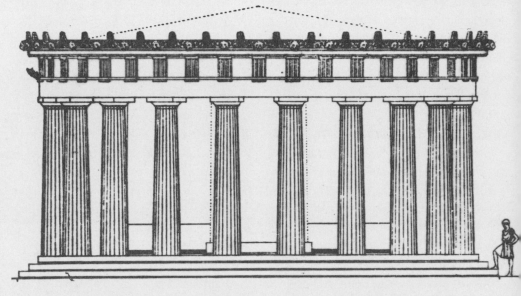

Above, plan of the Temple of Apollo. Right, reconstruction of the façade of the Treasury of Sicyon, an ancient city-state on the north coast of the Peloponnese. Left, reconstruction of the façade of the Treasury of Massilia (Marseilles).

Right, reconstruction of the tholos of the Sanctuary of Athena Pronaia. The temple was seriously damaged by two landslides, once in 480 B.C. and again in the twentieth century.

the two deities were eventually joined.

More radical religious changes at Delphi were later brought about by the people we now call Greeks, who were Dorian tribes migrating from Thessaly. They came down from the north at the end of the second millenium B.C. and imposed their language, their customs, and their gods on the country. Unlike the previous gods of Delphi, these new deities lived in the sky—not in the earth or the ocean. Their ruler was Zeus, who had married Themis. But it was Apollo who became the chief god at Delphi.

Apollo came from the island of Delos on the back of a dolphin. At Delphi he slew the serpent Python whom Gaea had ordered to guard the sanctuary. The dead Python then sank into a fissure in the earth where he lay stinking terribly. Inhaling this odor was thought to induce the oracular trance of the Delphic priestess.

Of the more than 250 oracles in the Greek-speaking world, Delphi was considered the most sacred and the most

reliable. Suppliants went to the shrine for answers to questions ranging from the personal and mundane to crucial matters of state. At first, the priestess would speak only once a year, on Apollo's birthday. Eventually, however, the crowds of pilgrims could approach the oracle during all but the winter months. Sometimes the god refused to answer, so before the priestess took her seat, cold water was poured over the head of a goat. If the animal trembled violently, it meant that the oracle would speak.

The priestess, or sibyl, was a free-born, middle-aged peasant woman of Delphi, who lived a blameless life. Her shrine was located in the *adytum,* or sanctum, below the Temple of Apollo, where the omphalos stone stood.

Suppliants followed a set performance at Delphi. Upon arriving at the sanctuary, they would register with the priests for an appointment. When the time came, the

suppliants paid their fees and joined together in a communal bath in the Castalian Fountain. The group then proceeded along the Sacred Way to the great altar outside the Temple of Apollo. Here, a garlanded sheep or goat was sacrificed, and the animal's entrails were carefully examined for omens. After the sacrificial ceremony, the suppliants entered the temple in turns to consult the sibyl.

Pythagoras, Socrates, Pindar, Aristotle, and Plato are only some of the famous figures of history who listened reverently to the words of the Delphic sibyl. The oracle preserved its reputation of infallibility by a carefully calculated obscurity. The answers of the priestess, which sometimes took the form of screaming and babbling, were translated by the priests of Apollo. Frequently, they were so vague as to be extremely misleading. When Croesus, King of Lydia in the sixth century B.C., asked the oracle if he should cross the river marking the border between his kingdom and Persia, the oracle replied: "If you do it, it will cause the downfall of a mighty country." Croesus crossed the river, was soundly defeated, and caused the downfall of his own country. There were many such incidents.

Regard for the Delphic oracle grew so great that Delphi actually became the cause of several sacred wars. In the sixth century B.C., the Phocians from central Greece tried to seize control of the rich Temple of Apollo. They were defeated by the Athenians, who then founded the Amphictyonic Council, a league of Greek city-states whose role was to maintain prescribed standards of conduct among its members and to guarantee the safety of the sanctuary at Delphi. To celebrate the Athenian victory, the Pythian games were established. These games, held every four years, were sacred to Apollo, and the victors were crowned with his laurel.

Delphi also played other roles in Greek life and politics. Lycurgus, the mythical lawgiver of Sparta, is said to have made his people swear that they would abide by his harsh new constitution for as long as he was away from Sparta. He then went to the Temple of Apollo at Delphi and stayed there until he died, insuring the permanent acceptance of the constitution. The Seven Sages of Greece, honored for their far-reaching contributions to Greek life and thought, were nominated by the Delphic oracle. Among those who received this honor were the Athenian legislator Solon and the philosopher Thales of Miletus. The wisdom of these sages was inscribed on the walls of Apollo's temple, including such formulas as "Know thyself" and "Nothing in excess."

Significant as the Temple of Apollo was, it was only one part of the sanctuary at

Above right, details of the façade of the Treasury of Massilia. The entablature is decorated with egg-and-dart moldings and with palmette, a pattern that also appears on the plaster capitals. The columns are an unusual variant of the Ionic order.

Right, reconstruction of the ancient Treasury of Sicyon, a round temple erected about 590 B.C.

Delphi. The entire complex covered over 200,000 square feet. Pilgrims who climbed from the port of Cirrha toward Mount Parnassus first came to an area which is now called Marmarià, the marble quarry, because its ruined temples were long pillaged for stone by later generations. Here was the first of the two great *temenoi,* or sacred precincts. It was dedicated to Athena Pronaia, "She who dwells before the temple." Athena was one of the most important divinities worshiped by the Greeks and, apart from Apollo, the only one to have her own temple at Delphi. Two different temples in the same precinct were dedicated to Athena at Delphi, the first built late in the seventh century B.C. and the second at the end of the sixth. Both are now destroyed. Between them stands an intriguing building called the *tholos.* The twenty Doric columns of this small, round structure enclosed a walled chamber, or cella, within which was another circular colonnade of ten Corinthian columns. Although probably religious in function, its specific use is not known.

Continuing upward, the path crosses a terrace where there was a gymnasium which the youths of Delphi used for sports and exercise. Beyond is the quiet and picturesque Castalian Fountain where pilgrims washed away their guilt before moving on to the upper sanctuary.

The upper sanctuary was a large temenos with the Temple of Apollo at its center. It was approached by the zigzagging Sacred Way, lined with treasuries (small storehouses), statues, and monuments from every city-state in Greece. Above the temple was the theater, and outside the temenos was the stadium, which was built for the Pythian games and could hold 7,000 spectators.

The monuments along the Sacred Way at Delphi formed a compendium of the history of Greek architecture. Corinth and Sicyon were the first to construct treasuries to celebrate victories and store their trophies. They were followed by Cnidus and Clazomenae, Potidaea, Athens, and even distant Massilia (Marseilles). And the people of the small island of Siphnos are only remembered now because of their elegant Ionic treasury at Delphi. Many of the treasuries no longer exist, although some have been laboriously reconstructed.

Clockwise from top left: archaeologist's drawing of the top, front, and sides of a cornice ornament with a lion's head drain spout, from the Syphnian Treasury; carved lotus and palmette frieze also from the Syphnian Treasury; drawing of an alabaster mussel found near the stoa of the Athenian Treasury. Probably from Phoenicia, this toilet article was ornamented with gold.

Among the finest works of art rescued from Delphi is the *Charioteer of Delphi—* one of the few original Greek bronzes to have survived.

After a glorious heyday, the oracle at Delphi gradually declined in importance, especially after Rome conquered Greece. Nero alone removed more than five hundred bronze statues from the sanctuary. In the fourth century A.D., the Roman Emperor Julian the Apostate attempted to restore the shrine, but the oracle responded with nothing more than a wail for the glory that once had been. Finally, in A.D. 390, Theodosius the Great—in the name of Christianity—closed the oracle, and the Temple of Apollo was razed to the ground by his successor Arcadius.

Mont-Saint-Michel

France

Preceding page, the abbey complex of Mont-Saint-Michel, seen from the northwest. The ancient abbey, with its thirteenth-century monastic block known as La Merveille (the Wonder) seen at the left, rises above an oak wood, which is all that remains of the forest of Scissy. The three final bays and the two-towered façade of the Romanesque church, which stood on the site of the present forecourt, were demolished in 1780. The modern causeway links the mountain to the town of Pontorson.

Left, the huge fortified abbey of Mont-Saint-Michel. Sturdy fifteenth-century ramparts encircle most of the base of the mountain. Within the walls, quaint houses—some dating from the fifteenth and sixteenth centuries—nestle closely together. Today, they serve mostly as hotels and souvenir shops.

Above, the reconstructed Romanesque crossing tower with its imaginatively restored Flamboyant spire. Dating from the 1890s, the spire blends harmoniously with late Gothic pinnacles of the apse.

Far left, a long flight of rampart steps that passes beneath an arch at the base of the polygonal Tour des Corbins, which is attached to the eastern end of La Merveille. The steps lead to two cylindrical towers of the châtelet, or gate house, that guards the main entry to the abbey.

Left, the southern range of buildings containing the abbot's apartments and guest lodgings, built by Abbot Tustin in the thirteenth century.

Below left, the Gabriel Tower, an impressive sixteenth-century addition to the mount's western ramparts. At that time, cannons were placed on raised platforms behind the casements.

A statue of the warrior-archangel Saint Michael, in the act of slaying a dragon, crowns the church's graceful spire (right). Saint Michael's outstretched wings are some 500 feet above sea level.

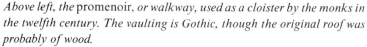

Above left, the promenoir, *or walkway, used as a cloister by the monks in the twelfth century. The vaulting is Gothic, though the original roof was probably of wood.*

Far left, a modern stained-glass window in the abbey church which depicts Saint Michael's sword protecting the Virgin and Child from a dragon. Left, a window in the fifteenth-century parish church.

Above, a crucifix, probably dating from the eleventh century, which stands in the cemetery of the parish church.

Top right, the Classical façade of the abbey church, added when the nave was shortened in 1780.

Center, the altar of Notre-Dame-sous-Terre (Our Lady under the Ground), a crypt chapel which is the oldest surviving part of the abbey complex.

Right, a head of Christ, preserved in the garden of the parish church. The abbey was used as a prison between the time of the French Revolution and 1863, and most of its statuary was destroyed during those years.

The cloister on the upper level of La Merveille (left) commands a superb view of sea and sky and flat lands. The slender columns support a staggered double arcade. The panels above the walkway side of the arches are decorated with delicate foliage carvings. The tiles on the roof are modern, having replaced the earlier lead roof. Below left, the enormous winch in the cellar of La Merveille, used for hauling up supplies.

Right, a triumph of airiness and elegance, the fifteenth-century choir of the abbey church is one of the finest examples of the Flamboyant Gothic style in France. Despite the intricately carved tracery which screens the lower windows, the overall effect is one of simplicity.

Below near right, the Guests Hall, which may once have been used to accommodate important pilgrims. Among those who visited Mont-Saint-Michel were Louis IX, Louis XI, and Francis I.

Below far right, the Knights Hall, so called because it was the nominal assembly hall of the Knights of Saint Michael. Louis XI created this order in 1469 to commemorate the abbey's strenuous resistance to English invasion. The lighting, detail, and perfect proportions of the chamber make it perhaps the most magnificent room in the abbey, after the choir of the church.

Following page, Mont-Saint-Michel, silhouetted against the sunset.

Mont-Saint-Michel France

Few buildings seize the imagination as strongly as the Abbey of Mont-Saint-Michel. It stands improbably perched on a rocky islet that rises 250 feet out of the sea, just off the coastal flat lands of north-western France, opposite the Normandy-Brittany border. Twice a day, the tide recedes over the sands and quicksands of Mont-Saint-Michel Bay and then rushes back—sometimes faster, according to local lore, than a galloping horse. At high tide the only link to the mainland is a narrow causeway of recent construction.

Mont-Saint-Michel has been many things over the centuries: a monastery, a church, a fortress, a prison, a center of learning, and even the seat of a chivalric order. In the Middle Ages, pilgrims flocked here from all over Europe to seek the blessing of the warrior-archangel Saint Michael, in whose honor the abbey was built. Some of them drowned on the last leg of their journey. The present-day pilgrims, however, are tourists, for whom the abbey remains one of the principal attractions of France.

Before the eighth century, the island of Mont-Saint-Michel, like the smaller island of Tombelaine one mile to the north, was still part of the mainland, a rocky hill surrounded by the vast forest of Scissy. In pagan times the Celts worshiped the god Belenus there, and later it was a center for the Roman worship of Jove. In the fifth century, Cornish hermits took possession of both summits and constructed shrines, one to Saint Stephen, first martyr of the Christian church, and one to a local martyr, Saint Symphorian.

Legend has it that in 708, Aubert, the bishop of the nearby town of Avranches, had a series of dreams in which the archangel Michael commanded him to build an oratory on the summit of Mont-Saint-Michel. Aubert obediently built a round, cryptlike church—said to accommodate about a hundred worshipers—slightly

The archangel Michael appeared in three dreams to Bishop Aubert, commanding him to build a shrine on the rock of Mont-Saint-Michel. This illustration (above) from a twelfth-century manuscript shows the archangel tapping the bishop on the head to remind him.

Right, an evocative and reasonably accurate representation of Mont-Saint-Michel, taken from one of the most renowned of medieval manuscripts, "Les très riches heures du duc de Berry." The façade and final three bays of the church were later demolished.

Below, the archangel Michael, conqueror of Satan. He was often depicted in Christian art as a dragon slayer. The newly converted Normans put themselves under his powerful protection.

Right, a plan of the abbey complex at the level of the church, as it existed in the fifteenth century.

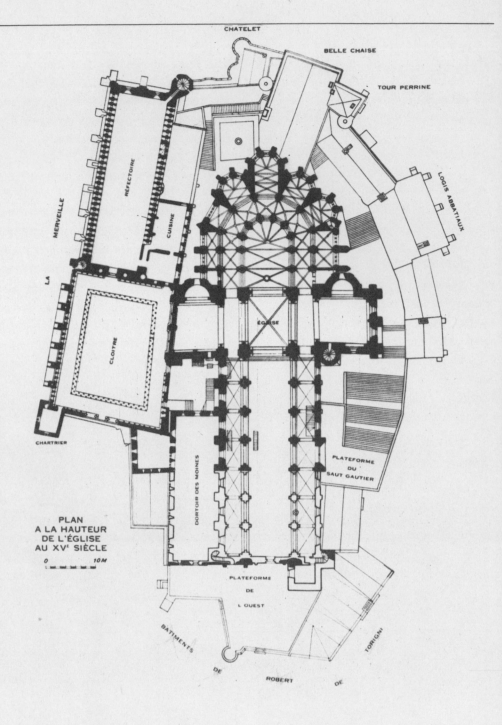

CHATELET

BELLE CHAISE

TOUR PERRINE

LOGIS ABBATIAUX

MERVEILLE

RÉFECTOIRE

CUISINE

LA

CLOÎTRE

ÉGLISE

CHARTRIER

DORTOIR DES MOINES

PLATEFORME
DU
SAUT GAUTIER

PLAN
A LA HAUTEUR
DE L'ÉGLISE
AU XVᵉ SIÈCLE

0   10M

PLATEFORME
DE
L'OUEST

BATIMENTS

DE

ROBERT

DE

TORIGNI

below and to the west of the apex of the rock. Here, he established a small Benedictine abbey. He then sent envoys to seek relics at Monte Gargano in southern Italy, the most famous of Saint Michael's hilltop shrines.

In 709, a freak tide, or perhaps a series of them, associated with a slight rise in the sea level, ripped out the forest of Scissy, so that the rocky hill became an island.

During the Viking raids of the ninth century, the island became a refuge for fleeing peasants, and a small town grew up below the colony of monks. As the Norse chieftains became Norman dukes, they took the shrine under their protection so that they, in turn, could enjoy the protec-

tion of the archangel Michael. In 966, Richard I, Duke of Normandy, expelled the twelve monks who served the shrine at that time, accusing them of laxity. He replaced them with Benedictines from two important monasteries in Normandy and from the one at Monte Cassino in Italy.

In 992, the second abbot of this new band of monks, Maynard II, began a new church on the top of the mount. At the same time, he rebuilt Bishop Aubert's oratory as a barrel-vaulted crypt, in which form it has survived to this day under the name of Notre-Dame-sous-Terre (Our Lady under the Earth).

The Norman dukes continued to take an increasing interest in Mont-Saint-

Michel, and its fame spread. In 1017, Richard the Good chose it as the site of his marriage to Judith of Brittany. Yet even the new church proved inconveniently small for the purpose. Probably on account of this, Richard contributed funds to a project conceived by Abbot Hildebert II to replace it with a large Romanesque church.

Hildebert's plan was both original and bold—perhaps a little too bold, since some centuries later large sections of his church either collapsed or had to be demolished. Owing to his refusal to sacrifice height by leveling the top of the mountain, only the crossing between the transepts and the first four bays of the nave could be built on solid rock. The chancel, the transepts, and the nave's three western bays were supported on multilevel crypts, many of which dated back to the 992 rebuilding of the church. The interior elevation of the surviving eastern half of the nave still displays the round arches, sturdy pillars, long wall shafts, and what the American historian Henry Adams called the "military poetry" of the early Romanesque style.

The abbey must have been generously funded, for despite the expense, the Abbot Ranulf was able to send six fully equipped ships to help bring Duke William the Conqueror back to Normandy after his

losing most of her French possessions. The abbey was besieged by Breton troops, who were allies of the French King Philip Augustus. They set fire to the town and damaged the north side of the abbey. The following year, Mont-Saint-Michel and Normandy passed to France, and the French king made reparations that enabled the Abbot Jourdain to undertake what was to become the most famous and spectacular part of the whole abbey complex—the three-storied, mostly residential wing aptly known as La Merveille (the Wonder).

La Merveille, which took twenty-five

years to build, is an outstanding example of early thirteenth-century monastic architecture. Standing close to the north side of the church, it has three floors, each divided into two halls. At the east end of the lowest level is the almonry, a long room with a vaulted ceiling supported by a row of thick, square columns. Next to it is the cellar, into which supplies for the abbey were hoisted from below. The cellar is wider than the almonry, with a double row of square piers that also support a vaulted ceiling.

The spacious and graceful rooms on the next floor are unmistakably Gothic.

Left, a detail from the Bayeux tapestry, which chronicles the Norman conquest of England. It depicts an incident in which some of William's knights, on a visit to Mont-Saint-Michel, got into difficulties in the quicksand around the abbey and had to be rescued.

Below, an eighteenth-century map of Mont-Saint-Michel Bay indicating the vast area swept by the tides.

successful invasion of England in 1066.

Under the learned Abbot Robert de Torigni (1154–1186), a friend and adviser of Henry II of England, Mont-Saint-Michel became known as the "City of Books" and was renowned as a center of learning. It also prospered materially, acquiring extensive properties in England, Normandy, and Brittany. De Torigni added a twin-towered, High Romanesque façade to the church as well as a range of administrative and residential buildings on its southwest side. Most of this work has unfortunately been destroyed.

In 1203, Mont-Saint-Michel was involved in the conflict between England and France which resulted in England

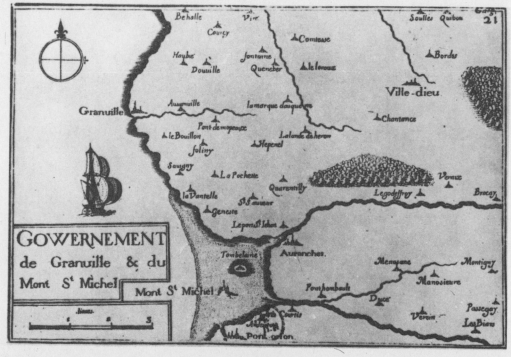

Above the almonry is the Salle des Hôtes (Guests Hall), where the pilgrims are thought to have stayed. This is an elegant room 115 feet long with a central row of slender pillars and a roof of Gothic rib vaulting. Opening off it is a small chapel that connects with one of the church crypts and a little terrace garden.

Above the cellar is the Salle des Chevaliers (Knights Hall), perhaps the grandest room in the whole abbey. This was the monks' scriptorium, or writing room. It was given its somewhat misleading name in 1469 when Louis XI made a pilgrimage to Mont-Saint-Michel and founded the chivalric Order of St. Michael there. The knights of the order, however, probably never met in the hall.

On the top floor, at the level of the church, are the refectory and cloister. The former, which has no interior columns, is an airy room filled with a diffused light, the source of which is invisible to anyone standing at either doorway. Light filters into the room from lancets cut into deeply recessed niches on both sides.

The west door of the refectory leads into the cloister, which was the last section of La Merveille to be built. Though it measures only some 85 by 45 feet, the cloister gives a stunning impression of spaciousness. The effect is mainly attributable to

Below, a seventeenth-century Flemish engraving of Mont-Saint-Michel. It emphasizes the impregnability of the abbey fortress and shows why it was called "In Peril of the Sea."

the unusual slenderness of the staggered double row of columns separating the cloister's central open space from the encircling walkway.

When the duchy of Normandy became a part of France, Mont-Saint-Michel acquired some strategic importance. Abbot Tustin received a handsome grant from Louis IX to strengthen the mountain's insufficient outer defenses. By the beginning of the fourteenth century, Mont-Saint-Michel was protected by a permanent garrison under the abbot's command.

Mont-Saint-Michel was such a popular shrine that even the Hundred Years' War (1337–1453) did not deter pilgrims from visiting the monastery. To do so, they were obliged to pay a fee to the English, who held the surrounding region for much of this period. Though the abbey itself was often besieged, it was never taken. In fact, its spirited independence had become legendary soon after 1425, when 120 knights withstood the assault of 8,000 English troops.

In 1421, the crypt beneath the old Romanesque chancel collapsed, bringing the chancel down with it. Repairs, delayed because of the war, were carried out between 1452 and 1521. Considering its late date, the new crypt (Crypte des Gros Piliers) is surprisingly austere. Its ten massive piers have no capitals, and the soaring new chancel—though the most decorated part of the abbey—is still relatively restrained. The chancel is built in the Flamboyant style. The flying buttresses that

support the chancel vaulting from the outside are especially spectacular.

Though Mont-Saint-Michel played a role in the religious wars of the sixteenth century, its days of glory were by then over. Few pilgrims visited the abbey. The abbots had become venal and the monks undisciplined. In 1622, the monks were expelled and replaced by others from the Congregation of Saint Maur, a recently founded Benedictine order dedicated to scholarship and teaching. The new monks revitalized the abbey's religious life. They lacked money, however, for the extensive repairs that were by that time needed for the church and the monastery.

The French Revolution brought monastic life to a halt at Mont-Saint-Michel, as it did throughout France. The monks were driven out and the abbey's properties were sold. Some of its splendid halls were partitioned off for prison cells, a function they retained until 1863.

In 1874, the abbey was classed as a historic monument and came under the protection of the state. Major restoration work was undertaken, some of it in the style of prevailing taste. The most unfortunate restorations, however, have since been "unrestored."

Today, after contending for centuries with fires, wars, tempests, structural collapse, and "restoration," Mont-Saint-Michel can still evoke the atmosphere of its spiritual heyday. A few monks are even permitted to live in the abbey—provided they don't interfere with the tourist trade.

MONT S.: MICHEL.

Campo dei Miracoli of Pisa

Italy

Preceding page, the grassy Campo dei Miracoli, or Field of Miracles, located close to the old city walls of Pisa, showing the circular baptistery (top center); the Cathedral of Santa Maria Maggiore (center right); the Campo Santo, or cemetery building (top right); and the campanile, or bell tower, better known as the Leaning Tower (bottom). The four buildings, all of pure white marble accentuated by dark green marble, are remarkable for the unity of their design. Though construction took three hundred years, each successive architect remained loyal to the graceful themes, including the blind arcades and pillared galleries, established by Buscheto, the original architect. The Field of Miracles itself is unusual, for though it is a cathedral square, it is neither paved nor at the town center. Rather, it nestles against the ancient defensive walls (visible at the top and right side of the picture) that once defined the city's limits.

Left, the cathedral baptistery and Campo Santo, as seen from the Leaning Tower.

Below left, the baptistery, with the cathedral, Campo Santo, and the Leaning Tower beyond. Over the centuries, architects were able to endow each building with distinct character while maintaining the balance of the whole.

Right, the Leaning Tower of Pisa. Work on this bell tower began in 1174. By the time the first three tiers had been completed a century later, the instability of the ground underneath the tower had caused it to lean. No correction was made until after the fourth level had been built. The upper tiers were then "bent" to bring them closer to the vertical.

Admired above all for the harmonious elegance of its ornamentation, the cathedral of Pisa (above) is considered the finest example of Italian Romanesque architecture. Though its plan is similar to that of other Romanesque churches, it is more monumental, and its transept arms, each with its own apse, are unusually long.

Above left, the apse of the cathedral. Left, detail of the façade. These two parts of the cathedral—the last to be built aside from the dome—first employed the arcade screening motif which links the church, tower, and baptistery.

All but one of the original bronze doors of the cathedral's façade—the work of Bonanno Pisano—were destroyed by the fire in 1595. They were replaced by bronze doors (left), designed by Raffaele Pagni, a follower of the Mannerist sculptor Giambologna. The center door depicts the life of the Virgin, to whom the church is dedicated, and the side doors illustrate the life of Christ.

Facing page, panels from the one remaining door by Bonanno Pisano, dating from about 1180. It stands in the portal of Saint Ranieri in the south transept, the closest to the heart of the city and the one entrance generally used by worshipers. The panels of the door depict scriptural scenes that are effectively suggested by just a few simple figures and some architectural or natural elements—a technique not unlike sketching in bronze. The style of the door is reminiscent of Byzantine mosaic art. Above right, the Magi. Right, the Nativity. Far right, clockwise from upper left, the Temptation of Christ, the Transfiguration, the Flight into Egypt, the Two Marys, the Annunciation, the Circumcision. Bottom, the Apostles.

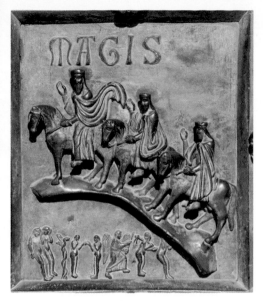

MAGIS

ERAT AD DIABOLU

TRANSFIGURATIO

VACES EGIPTI IN DEO TEMPLI PLER

FUGE IN EGIPTU

TE MORI AGRAS VALENA

STALL ABE

NATIVITAS DNI

ET OS NT P ACHBA P IN OT MIC

The awesome nave of the cathedral (facing page) leads the eye directly to the apse, with its beautiful mosaic depicting Christ enthroned between the Madonna and Saint John the Evangelist (1303). The nave was begun by Francesco di Simone and Vincenzo da Pistoia; Cimabue also worked on it. The coffered ceiling of the nave was the one concession made to contemporary taste during the reconstruction following the fire of 1595. Suspended from the ceiling is the bronze Lamp of Galileo. According to a dubious legend, its swaying inspired Galileo's theory of the pendulum. The masterpiece of the cathedral, and perhaps the finest sculptural work of the Italian Gothic, is the octagonal pulpit, seen on the left side of the nave, built by Giovanni Pisano between 1302 and 1310.

Right, the monolithic pillars that separate the nave from the aisles of the cathedral.

Below, the allegorical figure of Fortitude, from the pulpit.

Deceptively light and airy in appearance, the celebrated Leaning Tower (facing page and right) is a substantial hollow cylinder. Its six galleries echo the arcades on the façade of the cathedral. A spiral staircase with 293 steps leads to the terrace of the belfry. The climb is a singular experience, for the inclination of the tower gives one the sensation of continuous swaying motion.

The Renaissance art historian Vasari suggested that the inclination of the tower was the whim of the architect. The actual cause, however, is the instability of the ground on which it is built. In fact, there are other leaning towers in Pisa, though none are as famous. Now, nearly seven hundred years after it first started to lean, the tower inclines almost 14 feet from the vertical, a figure that increases by a fraction of an inch every year.

Below far right, the baptistery and cathedral seen through one of the upper colonnades of the tower.

Below right, the portal of Saint Ranieri in the south transept of the cathedral, seen from the doorway of the tower.

The baptistery (facing page) was begun in 1153 and completed in the late fourteenth century. Above, detail of the second-level arcade with its superimposed Gothic pinnacles and pediments. Left, part of the highly ornamented Gothic reconstruction above the second-level arcade. The arcade is further enriched by sculpted busts of saints and prophets—produced by Nicola and Giovanni Pisano and their followers. These are copies. Some of the originals have been moved to the National Museum in Pisa, while others are inside the baptistery itself.

Following page, the dome of the baptistery, seen from within. In the late thirteenth century, the original roof of the building was altered. The base of the original vault was later surrounded by a dome, and the oculus in its center, which had been open to the sky, was covered by a smaller dome. The larger, lower dome served an aesthetic rather than a structural function. By accommodating an additional story with twenty large windows, the dome markedly improved the lighting of the interior.

The interior of the baptistery is severely monumental (above right). Within its thick, smooth wall is a circular arcade of eight columns interspersed with four great piers, surmounted by a second arcade, that of the women's gallery (left). A tall, cylindrical space is formed, in the center of which stands the baptismal pool, executed in 1246 by Guido Bigarelli da Como. Nicola Pisano's pulpit (far right) is the masterpiece of the baptistery and a major sculptural work of thirteenth-century Italy. In one of its panels (right) showing the Nativity, the figure of Mary recalls the image of Phaedra on the Roman sarcophagus used for the burial of Beatrice of Canossa. Nicola's depiction of human figures is serene, Classical, and dignified, especially when compared to the stiff figures of much Romanesque sculpture. In contrast, the Madonna and Child (above), executed a generation later by Giovanni Pisano, shows a still more lifelike, less idealized conception of human form.

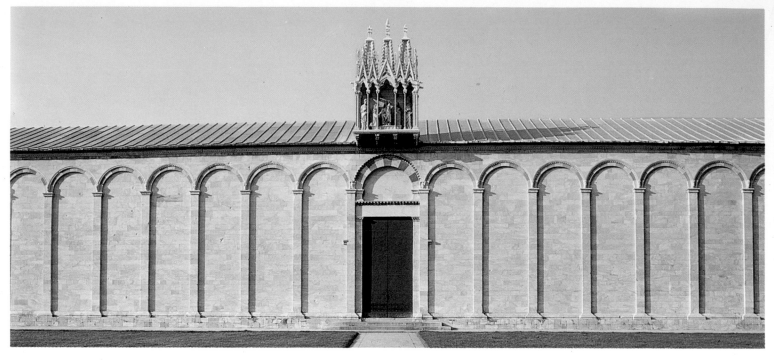

A marble wall of forty-three blind arches (above) closes off the north side of the Field of Miracles. The wall surrounds the Campo Santo, the cloistered cemetery begun by Giovanni di Simone in 1278 and completed at the end of the century. Over the door is a Gothic tabernacle (below left) with a marble group of the Madonna and saints, executed by the school of Giovanni Pisano.

Below right, a portion of the Roman wall and the Porta del Leone (Gate of the Lion) near the Campo Santo. Outside the wall is an old cemetery.

The cloister of the Campo Santo (facing page, below) is an arcade of round Romanesque arches, filled with elegant Gothic tracery. Above, the lawn within the cloister—the Campo Santo itself—which was at one time the burial place for commoners. The tombs and monuments of the nobility line the rear walls of the cloister and pave its floors.

Through the centuries, the Campo Santo has been enriched with works of art. Plaques and tombs are set into the walls of the cloister (top and bottom left). In the Ammanati Chapel is the Madonna with Child *by Giovanni Pisano (above), which once stood over the portal of Saint Ranieri. Center left, a bas-relief found in the Campo Santo.*

The Campo Santo's magnificent frescoes were virtually destroyed during an Allied attack in 1944. The most famous, now painstakingly restored, is the fourteenth-century Triumph of Death *(details, above right and near right). Also in the southern arcade are frescoes executed by Spinello Aretino between 1390 and 1392 (far right).*

Following page, the façade of the cathedral, with the Leaning Tower in the background.

Campo dei Miracoli of Pisa Italy

Mention Pisa, and most people immediately think of the legendary Leaning Tower. But mention Pisa to someone who has been there or is familiar with architectural history, and a different image springs to mind: a harmonious quartet of buildings—the Cathedral of Santa Maria Maggiore, the baptistery, the Campo Santo (a cloistered cemetery), and the bell tower, better known as the Leaning Tower—which together represent the high point of Italian Romanesque architecture.

The lawn itself is called the Campo dei

Miracoli—the Field of Miracles. Unlike most medieval cathedral squares, the Field of Miracles lies not in the city's center but at its edge, alongside a defensive wall that dates from Roman times. The grassy lawn is also distinctive because it is the only cathedral square in Italy that is not paved. Above all, the Field of Miracles is renowned for its "miraculous" tower that has been threatening to fall for seven hundred years. But it is perhaps equally miraculous that its four buildings, constructed over the course of several centuries, should complement each other and their surroundings so elegantly. With their graceful, almost Classical proportions of dazzling white marble striped and accented with dark green, the buildings have been compared to movements in a symphony of rhythmic and delicately carved arcades.

Throughout history, the absence of natural harbors along the flat Tyrrhenian coast of central Italy has conferred value on even the smallest, most insignificant inlet. Although Pisa was not situated on

the ocean, its location near the mouth of the Arno made it suitable for an inland, estuary port. By the early Middle Ages, Pisa had become a major center of trade because of its location at the juncture of the river and an ancient Roman road. A wealthy, independent republic, Pisa was an important port of call for pilgrims and dignitaries from the north or west traveling to Rome and for Syrian merchants sailing west.

As early as the ninth century, Pisan ships had ventured as far abroad as the coast of Africa, and the Pisan fleet had constituted the main Christian force of the Italian states in their battles with the Saracens. At first, the military aims of the Pisans were defensive. Among their principal victories were the defense of the southern Italian city of Salerno (871), the

Below, plan of Pisa made in 1797, three centuries after it had lost its political independence and more than seven centuries after the cathedral had been begun. The cathedral is near the upper left-hand corner.

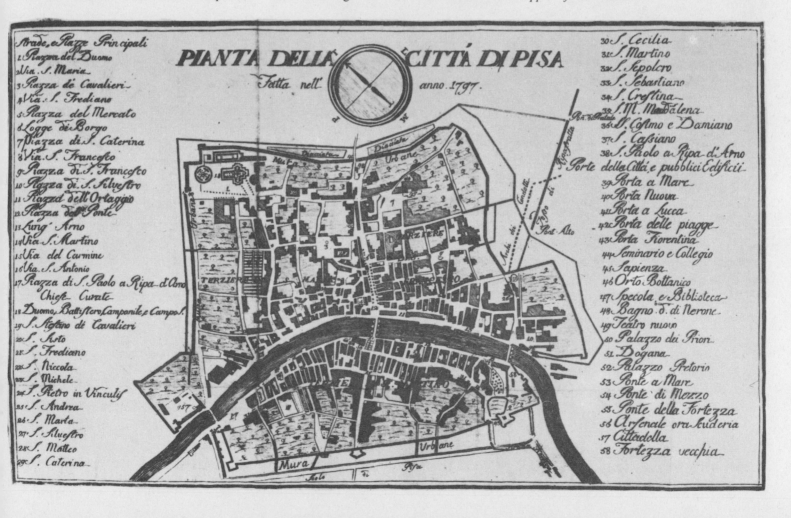

Piazza del Duomo di Pisa

Ponte di mezzo della Cittá di Pisa

These eighteenth-century prints depict the Field of Miracles (left) and the Ponte di Mezzo (below left). On the first Sunday in June, the Ponte di Mezzo is the scene of a traditional popular contest. Two teams from the two districts of the city, Tramontana and Mezzogiorno, which are separated by the Arno, compete to push a heavy cart into the opponent's zone.

fact, the cathedral represents both the beginning and the culmination of Pisan architecture. It combines a richness of material, a generosity of spatial relationships, and a Classical restraint of forms, grafted onto Romanesque-Lombardic roots. The final effect—the cold white marble against the luxurious expanse of green lawn—is extraordinarily beautiful.

The original architect of the cathedral—Buscheto—is named in inscriptions and official documents. In 1118, Pope Gelasius II consecrated the still unfinished church. The façade, with its superimposed arcading, was begun later in the twelfth century by a man named Rainaldus and completed by Guglielmo, who also executed the pulpit (1160) and the apse. Although the cathedral was extended beyond its original size and remained under construction intermittently for centuries, it shows a remarkable fidelity to its original spirit and motifs. The dome was finally completed about 1380, considerably later than the rest of the building, at the height of the High Gothic. Only here is there even a suggestion of changing sensibilities.

When, in the latter half of the twelfth century, a baptistery was planned to go up beside the unfinished cathedral, Pisa was at the height of its power. The city's population was about twenty-five thousand, a sizable figure in those days. In 1077, the pope had ceded Corsica to Pisa—although this did nothing to lessen the rivalry between Pisa and Genoa for control of the island. The First Crusade and other forays into territories from Tunisia to Asia Minor had provided the city with enormous amounts of treasure. Rich spoils were also taken in the victorious expedition against the Balearïc Islands (1113–1114), whose Arab sovereigns were brought back to Pisa as prisoners. The emperor of Byzantium,

defeat of the Arabs in the waters off Reggio di Calabria (1005), and the expulsion of the Saracens from Corsica and Sardinia (1015). These last were accomplished in cooperation with the Genoese, with whom the Pisans then struggled for control of these islands throughout the following two centuries.

Pisa subsequently took the offensive, carrying out increasingly bold and lucrative raids on Arab strongholds. Finally, in 1063, while helping the Normans under Robert Guiscard in their conquest of Sicily, Pisa attacked the Moslem city of Palermo, capturing six vessels laden with merchandise and sacking the city and its surroundings. The plunder was immense.

The citizens of Pisa, naturally enough, were eager to display the wealth and power of their city. To the medieval mind, there was no more fitting showcase for civic pride than a magnificent new church. In this spirit, the citizens of Pisa determined to build a cathedral in honor of no less a patron than the Virgin Mary herself. Construction of the church began in about 1089, close to the ancient battlemented walls of the town. The location of the cathedral suggests that the ambitious Pisans desired to break with tradition and look ahead to the expansion of their city.

Construction lasted three hundred years, during which time the original plan inevitably underwent modifications. In

Right, the sea defenses of the medieval port of Pisa. Silt washed down by the river created problems for the port as early as the twelfth century, gradually making it unusable. The Arno now flows into the sea about seven and a half miles beyond the city.

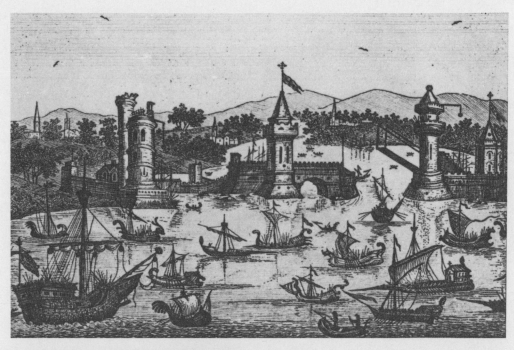

Below, the Torre Ghibellina, also known as the Torre di Sant'Agnese, which stands near the ancient city walls.

and erratic. In addition, the rivalry of Genoa and the jealousy of other Tuscan cities, especially Lucca and Florence, were becoming increasingly evident. But Pisa, in full expansion, ignored these warning signs.

In 1153, sixteen years after the defeat of Amalfi, work began on the baptistery of Pisa. The project was entrusted to a certain Diotisalvi, about whom little is known, though his name ("God save you") suggests that he was a foundling. He was heavily influenced by the original architect of the cathedral, Buscheto, as is evidenced by the arcading that encases the base of the baptistery, echoing the characteristic feature of the cathedral's façade. Inside, there is a circular colonnade modeled on the monumental colonnades that separate the aisles of the church. But the baptistery as it stands today is no longer as the Pisans first knew it. When completed, it had two identical arcaded upper stories, both like the still extant second story. The structure was capped by a severe conical roof which precisely reflected the shape of its open-topped conical dome.

Soon, however, Nicola Pisano was commissioned to rebuild the third story so that the windows there could be enlarged and the inconvenient open oculus—like that of the Roman Pantheon—in the center of the dome could be closed. In doing this, he added the nonstructural, round dome

who had granted the Pisans a district of their own in Constantinople, was paying the cathedral a tribute of four hundred gold pieces and two silk altar cloths each year. And Henry V, the Holy Roman Emperor (1111–1125), allotted the income from extensive lands in the area of the nearby city of Livorno to the construction of the cathedral.

The sack of Palermo and, above all, the defeat of the rival Italian republic of Amalfi in 1137 further enriched the already overflowing Pisan treasury. Frederick Barbarossa, Holy Roman Emperor (1155–1190), granted Pisa complete sovereignty over an extensive territory stretching from Portovenere, 35 miles to the

north of the city, to Civitavecchia, some 125 miles to the south. In time, Pisa established trading posts throughout the length and breadth of the Mediterranean. Favored everywhere by privileges and exemptions, these trade centers channeled a steady stream of gold back to the Pisan republic.

By the second half of the twelfth century, however, a number of critical difficulties had arisen. The port at Pisa no longer sufficed—due in part to silting of the river and a slight change in sea level. Another port, Porto Pisano, situated between Pisa and Livorno, had been built to supplement it. Communications between the new port and the city were inefficient

from which the original conical one now protrudes. He also began the Gothic decoration of the heightened third story. His design was eventually completed by his son Giovanni.

In 1174, shortly after work was begun on the baptistery, the architect and sculptor Bonanno Pisano was commissioned to design a bell tower for the cathedral. As the third story of this campanile was going up, in about 1298, there were disturbing indications that the ground beneath the structure was unstable. Work was halted repeatedly. The Pisans, already beset by troubles abroad, regarded the problem of the tower as an omen and a challenge. The campanile was finally completed under the direction of Giovanni di Simone. He attempted to correct the visual impression and the physical imbalance by angling the upper stories somewhat to bring them closer to the vertical. As a result, not only does the tower lean precariously, but its axis is slightly bent. The belfry atop the campanile was completed by Tommaso di Andrea in the second half of the fourteenth century.

The fourth and final building on the Field of Miracles was the cloistered cemetery called the Campo Santo, which was begun in 1278. Giovanni di Simone designed it to house the tombs that were scattered about the cathedral and to provide a stately and solemn resting place for those in the future who would most deserve commemoration. Ironically, the Campo Santo anticipated a heroic future for the city that was never to be realized.

About the time that the campanile started to lean, Pisa's fortunes began to decline. At the naval Battle of Meloria in 1284, the city suffered a defeat at the

hands of its rival, Genoa, from which it never fully recovered. Pisa also fell victim to the factional struggles between the popes and the Holy Roman emperors that beset Italy during this period. Weakened further by rivalry with the neighboring city of Lucca, by efforts to oppose Florentine expansion, and by the continuing struggle with Genoa for maritime supremacy, Pisa first lost its foreign territories and then its independence. Finally, in the fifteenth century, the city yielded to the domination of Florence.

The Italian Romanesque style, exemplified by the cathedral of Pisa, was rooted firmly in Italy's Classical tradition. Accordingly, the plan of the cathedral is essentially that of an early Christian basilica, transformed into the shape of a Latin cross by the addition of two transept arms, each with an apse of its own. The centerpiece of the Field of Miracles, the church is an imposing structure 325 feet long, 115 feet across at the nave, and 110 feet high.

All the main characteristics of the church—the huge colonnades of the nave and aisles, the arcading of the exterior—possess a marked unity of style. Buscheto, the cathedral's first architect, created the essentials of the building, which were then developed by his successors. He combined the most diverse qualities—Lombardic, Arabic, even an echo of the architecture of Armenia—with the spirit of Italian Classicism. The serenity of the cathedral's lines, its pillars and capitals that recall late

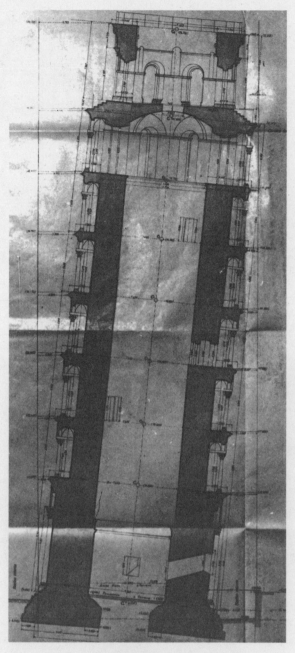

Left, vertical cross section through the tower. The ever-present threat of the tower's collapse stimulated many suggested remedies. One tongue-in-cheek proposal (below left) envisioned propping it up with a statue depicting its designer, Bonanno Pisano.

Far left, engraving made in 1782 showing the Leaning Tower of Pisa. Work on the tower was halted when, after the third story had been built, the settling of the ground began to cause the structure to incline. The upper three stories were added under the direction of Giovanni Pisano. The belfry, by Tommaso di Andrea Pisano, was begun about 1350 and completed about twenty-two years later.

Left, an early twentieth-century photomontage preserved in the Museum of the Opera Primiziale, purporting to represent a medieval proposal for adding four more stories and a conical roof to the tower originally planned by Bonanno Pisano.

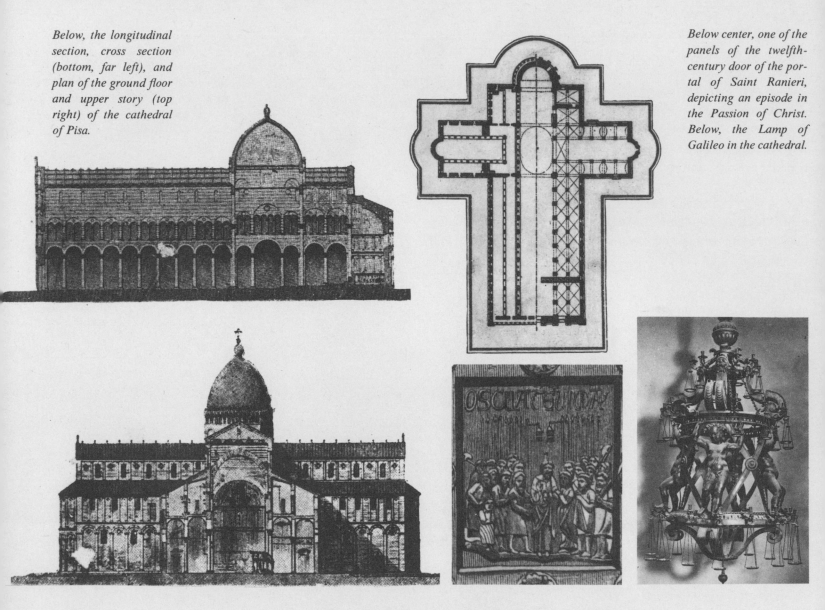

Roman basilicas, the spacious and unhurried rhythms of the major arcades—these all invoke the spirit of the ancient world. Within this Classical framework, however, there is the new sense of space: in the repetition of the lesser arcades, in the intersection of the transept with the body of the church, and in the elliptical plan of the dome itself.

In 1595, a fire, possibly caused by a careless worker repairing the lead roof, seriously damaged the nave. During the rebuilding, the only concession made to the taste of the time was the richly wrought, coffered ceiling of the nave, which the Florentine Atticiati substituted for the original exposed structural roof trusses. The fire also destroyed the three late twelfth-century bronze doors of the façade, cast by Bonanno Pisano. They were replaced in about 1603 with new bronze doors by Raffaele Pagni, who was a disciple of the Mannerist sculptor Giambologna. The one remaining door by Bonanno, on the portal of Saint Ranieri in the south transept, is distinctive both for its originality and its beauty. Yet the later doors in no way upset the harmony of the building.

The interior of the cathedral was embellished with precious works of art. The pulpit, executed by Giovanni Pisano between 1302 and 1310, is outstanding—just as the finest work in the baptistery is the pulpit completed fifty years earlier by his father, Nicola Pisano. Giovanni's pulpit is thought to be his most masterful piece of sculpture. Many, in fact, consider it the most important sculptural work of the Italian Gothic. Octagonal in design, it rests on nine supports, pillars alternating with carved allegorical figures. The panels on its sides depict scenes from the New Testament with a passion and intensity that had not yet been seen in Italian sculpture.

In the center of the church hangs the Lamp of Galileo, the famous bronze lamp made in 1587 from a model by Battista Lorenzi. According to tradition, the great scientist, a native of Pisa, formulated his theories about the swinging of a pendulum while gazing at the movements of the lamp during tedious church services. Though the legend has its charm, it is probable that Galileo had already made his discoveries by the time the lamp was put in place.

The cathedral's decoration includes paintings by Andrea del Sarto and Domenico di Pace Beccafumi and richly carved, wood choir stalls, which are the work of the fifteenth-century sculptor Guiliano da Maiano and his successors.

Though the baptistery was begun in

1153, nearly seventy years after the cathedral, it remained faithful to the overall spirit and the principal decorative design motif—the arcades, both blind (i.e., filled in) and otherwise—that were established so elegantly by the latter. With its added Gothic exterior decoration, it is the most elaborate of the group of buildings. Yet, the pediments, pinnacles, niches, and cusps do not seriously detract from the serenity of the baptistery. The dimensions of the circular building—115 feet in interior diameter and 180 feet to the top of the conical dome—harmoniously complement those of the church.

The internal plan of the baptistery follows the Classical scheme of a central ring of arcaded piers and columns with another arcaded gallery above. Its simplicity provides an elegant backdrop for the font, the altar, and the sculptured pulpit. The octagonal font, dating from 1248, is the work of Guido Bigarelli da Como, and the altar is made of twelfth-century carved panels that once decorated the balustrade of the cathedral presbytery.

Nicola Pisano's pulpit, completed in 1269, is the masterpiece of the baptistery. Hexagonal in design, the pulpit is borne on seven pillars, some supported on lions. Small trefoil arches link the pillars and support the five panels of the parapet. While his son's pulpit was modern, the panels of Nicola's pulpit are quietly Classical, almost antique, with none of the stiffness typical of Romanesque sculpture.

The campanile repeats the basic decorative motif of the cathedral and baptistery. One hundred eighty feet in height, the lacy cylinder is decorated with blind arcading at its base. Six tiers of airy arcaded galleries culminate in a belfry, and a spiral staircase set into the walls provides access to each level.

The tower is, of course, famous not because of the elegance of its conception—so frequently overlooked—but because of a single accident. Pisa's notorious Leaning Tower inclines almost fourteen feet from the vertical, a figure that increases by a small fraction of an inch every year. Some pessimists have even predicted the mo-

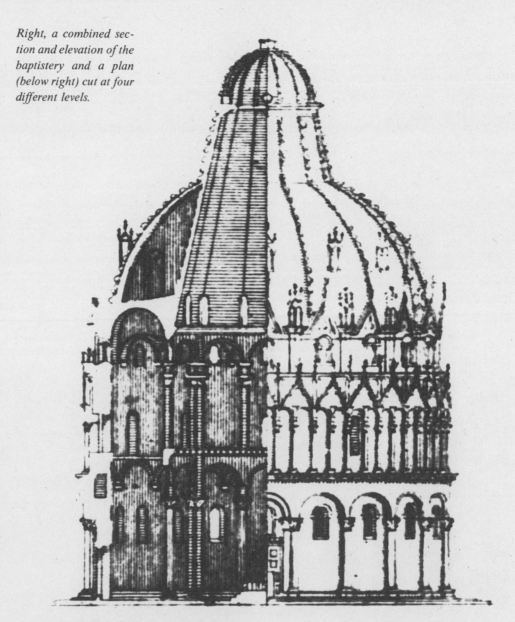

Right, a combined section and elevation of the baptistery and a plan (below right) cut at four different levels.

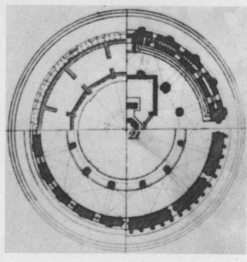

Basso rilievo nella Porta Orientale del Batistero Pisano

Left, engraving of one of the bas-reliefs of the east door of the baptistery.

ment when it must inevitably fall, while optimists the world over continue to provide suggestions for shoring up the structure and avoiding collapse.

For centuries, Pisan children have amused themselves by dropping stones from the top of the tower. According to legend, this pastime inspired Galileo's first investigations of the nature of gravity. There is, however, probably no more truth to this story than to the myth surrounding the lamp in the cathedral.

While the campanile has survived for seven centuries as one of the world's most precariously balanced monuments, the Campo Santo, the last of the four structures built on the Field of Miracles, has suffered irreparable damage. On July 27, 1944, artillery set fire to the wooden structure of the cemetery roof. As a result, molten lead poured down into the interior, baking and crumbling the plaster of its famous frescoes. Though much has been restored, the original glory of the Campo Santo can never be recovered.

Of the quartet of buildings in the Field of Miracles, the Campo Santo, begun in 1278, is most heavily influenced by the prevailing Gothic style. Its smooth, almost blank, exterior is very slightly articulated by the generously scaled shallow relief of its blind arcading. Light plays over the surface as on a long opalescent ribbon.

This great cloister, measuring 420 by 145 feet, closes off the north side of the Field of Miracles. Inside is a long lawn open to the sky, with a cypress tree at each corner. The earth of the lawn is said to have been brought from the Holy Land as ballast in the holds of Pisan ships. At one time, the lawn was the burial place for commoners. Tombs, sarcophagi, and monuments of noble families are set out beneath the arcades of the surrounding cloister, whose floor is completely paved with gravestones.

On the walls are the restored frescoes executed by the greatest Tuscan artists of four centuries. The most famous, and most dramatic, is the allegorical *Triumph of Death,* attributed to the Pisan master Francesco Traini and thought to date from the mid-fourteenth century.

Nine hundred years ago, the tiny city-state of Pisa was a great commercial and political power and a center of considerable intellectual and artistic accomplishment. It was this enlightened environment that inspired the cathedral at Pisa. An astonishing aesthetic purity, sustained over the course of several centuries by many artists and artisans, kept the church and its attendant buildings faithful to the original conception. Though Pisa's moment of glory was comparatively brief, the Field of Miracles still speaks eloquently of a brilliant golden age.

Left, the Campo Santo, during the period of restoration that followed the burning of its timber roof during World War II.

Left, a preparatory sketch for a fresco depicting hell. The drawing was brought to light during the restoration of the Campo Santo.

Teotihuacán

Mexico

Preceding page, a panoramic view of the central mall which unites the chief architectural sites of the ancient city of Teotihuacán. Between 200 B.C. and A.D. 650, this was the center of the most important city in North America. In contrast to the more warlike Aztecs, who dominated central Mexico at the time of the arrival of the Spanish, the Teotihuacános were a largely pacific people who devoted themselves to agriculture, trade, and the arts. The mall's morbid name, the Avenue of the Dead, is not of Teotihuacáno origin. It was coined by the Aztecs who found the city in ruins and assumed that the heaps of rubble, the remains of the minor temples lining the mall, were tombs. This view from the 135-foot summit of the Pyramid of the Moon shows on the right the ceremonial mall which stretches for a mile and a half. In the center is the vast Pyramid of the Sun, which is 210 feet tall and is composed of over 1,300,000 cubic yards of stone and mortar. Visitors can climb to the summit, experiencing

the dizzying sensation of mounting a staircase designed so that the climber at the bottom cannot see the top. The present reconstruction, part of an extensive program begun in 1905, merely provides a partial idea of the pyramid's original splendor. It was once covered with brilliant red and white stucco.

Above left and left, two staircases of the Temple of Quetzalcoatl, the Feathered Serpent.

Above, the open ceremonial plaza, known as La Ciudadela, which surrounds the temple.

Right, the terrace and smaller monuments which abut the much less extensive square at the base of the Pyramid of the Moon.

Left and below left, the staircase of the Temple of Quetzalcoatl. Carved heads of the Feathered Serpent and the rain god, Tlaloc, line the ascent. As Lord of the Morning Star and the patron of learning and justice, Quetzalcoatl represents the gentler side of the Meso-American pantheon. His cult is believed to be ancient, and he was known, in some form, to most of the later Mexican Indian cultures. Even the Mayas, who lived far away in the jungles of the Yucatán and Guatemala, worshiped him under the name of Kukulkán.

The heads of feathered serpents, seen here, are the most literal symbols of Quetzalcoatl's nature, showing the union of the green and crimson quetzal bird and the coatl, or snake. In pre-Toltec times, the Feathered Serpent was often pictured in human form, sometimes in the act of emerging from the jaws of the bird-snake. Quetzalcoatl himself was neither a bird nor a serpent but the spirit of human hope which arises from these earthly origins.

Facing page, stone reliefs from the temple walls including stylized portraits of the rain spirit, Tlaloc, the earliest god known to have been worshiped at Teotihuacán. Other existing representations of Tlaloc show a tongue of maize emerging from his gaping mouth. Although Tlaloc, in his simplest form, was a fertility god, the Teotihuacános also thought of him as the god of human creativity, the source of artistic as well as physical abundance. Colorful pictures once covered the temple walls. Remnants of these paintings are still visible, but most of the paintings have been worn away since the abandonment of the city a thousand years ago.

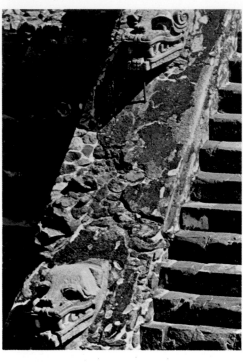

The inhabitants of Teotihuacán were noted craftsmen, specializing in stonework. Carved heads, such as those of the Feathered Serpent (left and right), were often ornamented with eyes carved from obsidian and semiprecious stones. Below, now-empty eye sockets of the Feathered Serpent look out over the partially reconstructed ruins of Teotihuacán. Beyond are the Pyramids of the Sun and Moon. Modern scholars suspect that the alignment and designs of the pyramids have an astrological significance.

Center right, shell decorations on the exterior of the Temple of Quetzalcoatl.

Bottom right, an exposed section of the temple's inner core. This rough building material, composed of volcanic rock, rubble, and mortar, was once covered with polished and painted plaster.

The Palace of Quetzalpapalotl (this page and above right) is one of the most exciting of the recent archaeological finds at Teotihuacán. Thought to have been the residence of the city's priest-ruler, it faces directly onto the courtyard of the Pyramid of the Moon. Its plan, similar to other palaces excavated in the city, includes secluded living quarters as well as an area ringed by deep, outdoor porches for public audiences.

Urban Teotihuacán was laid out in an orderly grid system, with blocks approximately 197 feet square. It was composed primarily of "apartment complexes," which consisted of family living quarters served by a unified drainage system, communal patios, and other centralized facilities, including shrines and cemeteries. The palaces and homes of the elite were closest to the city's religious center, with the dwellings of craftsmen and, finally, of peasants arranged in concentric circles beyond them. Apparently unconcerned with defense, the city had no walls or outer fortifications and simply extended its boundaries as the population grew.

Unfortunately, much of the history of these remarkable builders has been lost. In A.D. 650, Teotihuacán was sacked and burned by the Chichimecs, nomadic tribesmen so named because, to the civilized Indians of the central plateau, their speech sounded like a nonsensical babble of "chi-chi-chi." By the end of the ninth century, the city was abandoned, and soon after, the Teotihuacán Indians became extinct as a tribe. Modern scholars agree that the Teotihuacános left no heirs. Even the name by which we remember them comes from the Aztec language; not a single word of their native tongue is known.

Details of carvings from the Palace of Quetzalpapalotl (below right) are thought to represent the brilliantly plumed quetzal, once found throughout Mexico but now restricted to the southern jungles.

Following page, the Pyramid of the Sun. Both the central staircase and five terraces are twentieth-century reconstructions. In Aztec times the whole structure was half hidden under its own debris and vegetation, although the remains of the temple on the summit, now destroyed, may still have been visible. To Montezuma's people, this was a sacred place, the home of the gods. For contemporary Mexicans, it is a reminder that they are the heirs of 2,000 years of civilization.

Teotihuacán Mexico

Legend says that the sorrows of Mexico began with the fall from grace of the great god the Indians knew as Quetzalcoatl, the Feathered Serpent. Mild, just, and celibate, this god-king was a patron of learning and had been for centuries the guiding spirit of the Toltec empire, which rose to power in central Mexico from the tenth to the twelfth century A.D. Then, suddenly, fate turned against Quetzalcoatl. While enjoying a banquet, he allowed himself to become drunk and was seduced by the malevolent beauty of the goddess of the

magic mushroom. The next day he awoke to the knowledge that, through this moment of weakness, he had forfeited his claim to godhood. Repentant, Quetzalcoatl immediately gave up his kingdom, marched naked to the Gulf of Mexico, and vanished into the eastern sea.

A few centuries later, the realms of his people, the Toltecs, fell prey to invaders from the north. These were the Aztecs, who worshiped a far more warlike god called Huitzilopochtli (hummingbird-wizard). A military people, the Aztecs were devoted to their powerful but demonic god, pacifying him with thousands of hearts torn from live captives. The Aztecs also revered Quetzalcoatl as the patron of priests as well as the inventor of the calendar and of books. Someday, they believed, the Feathered Serpent would return from the east and the Aztec empire would fall, to be replaced by an era of peace and justice. Then, it was said, the gods would no longer demand blood sacrifices but would be satisfied with offerings

of fruit and flowers.

This prophecy remained unfulfilled until A.D. 1519, when the scholarly Aztec ruler Montezuma heard momentous news. A group of strange, white-skinned men, wearing clothes of iron and riding "hornless deer as tall as houses," had arrived on the eastern coast. Surely their leader was the great god Quetzalcoatl. When this unusual band of travelers reached Tenochtitlán, the island capital of the Aztecs, they were welcomed as gods.

The Spaniards, however, were far from divine. They decimated and enslaved the Indian population, tore down their monuments, and all but eradicated the history of Mexico's great pre-Columbian civilizations. Because of this wholesale destruction, later generations of Europeans saw the Indians of Meso-America as enigmas and dreamed up fanciful explanations for the existence of massive, ruined temples in such a primitive land. The true explanations of these buildings and the complex civilizations which created them remained buried in ruins for centuries.

It was not until the nineteenth century that Mexican scholars began to unearth the story of pre-Columbian Mexico's most impressive urban complex at Teotihuacán. Covering eight square miles and dominated by the massive Pyramid of the Sun, this city had been the center of Mexican

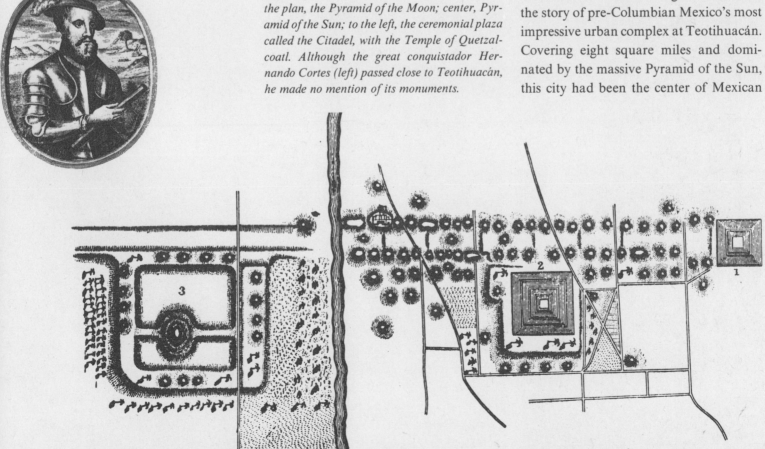

Below, plan of the temple complex of Teotihuacán prior to its excavation. To the right in the plan, the Pyramid of the Moon; center, Pyramid of the Sun; to the left, the ceremonial plaza called the Citadel, with the Temple of Quetzalcoatl. Although the great conquistador Hernando Cortes (left) passed close to Teotihuacán, he made no mention of its monuments.

Above, a Toltec stone plaque representing the rain god's mouth mask. The Toltecs dominated central Mexico from 750 to 1000 A.D. Below, a carved stele.

civilization from at least 200 B.C. to A.D. 650. It was already empty and half overgrown with vegetation when Cortes is said to have regrouped his forces in the shadow of Teotihuacán's great pyramids. The Aztecs had been using the abandoned site, thirty-three miles north of their own capital, as a place of pilgrimage. For Montezuma's people, Teotihuacán was the "burial place of kings" or, more picturesquely, "the place where the lords of the people awoke from the dream of life to become gods."

Teotihuacán was not originally built as a place of pilgrimage. At its height, it boasted between 100,000 and 150,000 inhabitants and was undoubtedly the largest city in North America. The religious monuments which so impressed the Aztecs were only one part of a major metropolis that anticipated many of our modern concepts of city planning.

The residents of Teotihuacán did not, for the most part, live in private homes but in "apartment complexes" housing between twenty and one hundred people. Each apartment had its own kitchen and facilities for storing rainwater. They even had a way of disposing of garbage by leaving it in a sort of back patio that the ubiquitous turkey buzzards would clean out. Each complex shared a shrine and a burial site, presumably for former occupants. All of the buildings were fashioned from a kind of concrete made of a volcanic rock called *teconite* mixed with gravel, clay, and mortar. The hardened mixture was covered with plaster which was polished until it acquired a watertight finish.

The structures excavated so far—more than 2,600—follow a grid plan reminiscent of modern city blocks. The palaces and apartments of the wealthy are clustered near the center of town. The whole complex was served by a surprisingly advanced system of municipal services, including reservoirs and drainage pipes. Unlike most ancient cities, Teotihuacán had neither walls nor outlying fortifications. Although the Teotihuacános traded all over Mexico and as far away as Kaminaljuyú in Guatemala, they seem to

have made few enemies and lived without fear of attack.

Their confidence was justified until nomadic invaders set fire to the city in A.D. 650. This disaster touched off a rapid decline that led to the total abandonment of Teotihuacán in about 900. Some historians have theorized that the true cause of the city's fall was not this invasion but the destructive effects of urban sprawl, including food shortages and a breakdown of municipal services. Whatever the reason, the Teotihuacáno civilization vanished from the face of the earth.

Who were these people who disappeared without leaving a single word of their language? For the most part, they remain a mystery, but remnants of their pottery, paintings, and carvings show that the Teotihuacános had achieved a high level of technical and artistic skill. Indeed, archaeologists estimate that one in every three or four citizens was an artisan. Many of this class worked at fashioning useful and beautiful objects from the obsidian that was mined nearby. This black volcanic glass, highly valued in Meso-America, was used for knives and razors, for lip ornaments, and in ceremonial objects of all kinds. Later, it was used in the highly polished mirrors used by Aztec priests for divination. Lapidary work was apparently a Teotihuacáno specialty. Yet, metal crafts, such as the gold and copper

work later practiced by the Aztecs, were unknown.

Another accomplishment of the Teotihuacános was the development of the wheel. Lacking suitable draft animals, however, they could find few practical applications for their discovery and used the wheel primarily in children's toys.

The Teotihuacános appear to have devoted their energies primarily to trade and craftsmanship. But they were also highly religious. As the city grew, so did the complex of religious monuments which

Below, Claude Joseph Charnay, who began unofficial excavations at Teotihuacán in the late nineteenth century. He mistakenly believed it to be a Toltec city.

Below, Teotihuacán as it appeared to its first excavators. A painting (below right) from the Temple of Agriculture, near the Pyramid of the Moon, depicts Teotihuacános sacrificing seeds to their gods.

marked its center. The earliest and most impressive of these monuments is the massive pyramid which the Aztecs later associated with the birthplace of the sun. Formed by covering a much smaller temple with successive layers of clay and rubble, this pyramid reached a height of 210 feet, resting on a rectangular base measuring about 720 by 760 feet. By the time it was finished in about A.D. 100, the structure contained some 1,300,000 cubic yards of building materials. Originally, the whole outer surface was covered with bright red and white stucco, and the summit of the pyramid was crowned with a small temple. The impulse behind this formidable project remains a mystery. Recent excavators, however, appear to have discovered an important clue: a tunnel under the pyramid's base that leads to a small natural cavern. It is thought that the Teotihuacános may have regarded this cavern as the home or birthplace of the principal god, the rain spirit Tlaloc.

Although Tlaloc was probably the first god of the city, he was certainly not the only important one. The civilizing influence of Quetzalcoatl was also very much present. The Feathered Serpent had not yet assumed the central position he would achieve under the Toltecs, who bestowed the name Quetzalcoatl on a series of their rulers. Among the Teotihuacános, who appear to have been governed by a priestly caste, the idea of the Feathered

Serpent as a beneficent ruler had probably not yet emerged. Nevertheless, his cult flourished in Teotihuacán, and it is said that here "the serpent learned to fly."

The Pyramid of the Sun stands along what the Aztecs called the Avenue of the Dead, a ceremonial mall that is one and a half miles long. At the northern end of this mall stands a smaller pyramid, 135 feet tall, named by the Aztecs as the Pyramid of the Moon. At the southern end of the avenue stands the Temple of Quetzalcoatl. Though far smaller than either of the pyramids, the temple is surrounded by a courtyard covering a full thirty-six acres. This courtyard must have been a major ceremonial plaza of metropolitan Teotihuacán; despite its present name—La Ciudadela, or the Citadel—it had nothing to do with defense. The Temple of Quetzalcoatl was reserved for coronations and for the observance of various holidays dictated by the city's astrologer-priests. It was apparently built later than the major pyramids, a possible indication that, as this peaceful and artistic culture evolved, Quetzalcoatl's virtues had begun to gain an ascendancy over the more elemental powers of the rain god Tlaloc.

The quetzal, the bird half of the Feathered Serpent's persona, is also found in the name of the recently excavated Quetzalpapalotl Palace, which stands at the northern end of the mall near the Pyramid of the Moon. This was probably the resi-

Left and right, two elaborate sculptures of Quetzalcoatl, the great Feathered Serpent. Below, Toltec terra-cotta masks. The Toltecs inherited the traditions of the peoples who flourished in central Mexico before them and who created Teotihuacán.

dence of the priest-ruler. The palace's carved relief figures are thought to represent the god's incarnation as a bird-butterfly.

Like the Aztecs, the Teotihuacános delved deeply into magic and into symbolic interpretations of dreams. Their gods were never static or severe idols, but shape-changers who came to them in constantly renewed guises. Religion was obviously of central importance, inspiring the best efforts of the city's astronomer-mathematicians, artists, and builders. However, this does not mean that their life was in any way joyless or restricting. Tlaloc, for example, was not envisioned merely as a demanding rain demon. To the Teotihuacános, he was also "the bearer of the luminous seed which converts matter into creative energy."

The modern visitor to Teotihuacán sees only the bare, monochrome stone figures that have been resurrected from the rubble of the centuries. Perhaps this is why many people today believe that pre-Columbian Mexican cultures were unrelievedly grim. But, just as the marble stat-

ues of Athens were once brightly painted, so too were the walls of Meso-American temples painted and adorned with obsidian eyes and other precious and colorful ornamentation.

Teotihuacán, in particular, must have been a bustling place, enlivened by the presence of so many craftsmen and foreign traders. The gloomy names now associated with its religious monuments are not authentic. The Avenue of the Dead, for example, is so called because the Aztecs mistook the rock-strewn mounds of minor temples for tombs.

In Mexico itself, the notion that the great Indian cultures are dead and irrelevant has been strongly challenged by the twentieth-century heirs of the nationalist revolution. Modern excavations of Teotihuacán, which began officially in 1905 and are still far from complete, are providing modern Mexicans with a symbolic link with their Indian ancestors. For Mexican poets and artists, the physical survival of this Indian stonework has been an inspiration. Quetzalcoatl still lives; though he is no longer a godlike savior who will appear

out of the east. He represents the healing spirit which must arise from within to resolve the violent struggles of Mexico's past. This longing for inner peace is expressed by the Mexican poet Octavio Paz in his poem, "Hymn Among the Ruins":

Night falls over Teotihuacán.
On top of the pyramid the boys smoke marijuana,
they play their harsh guitars.
What grass, what water of life will
give us life, where shall we dig up
the buried word, the proportion that
sustains the hymn and the discourse,
the dance, the city, the balance? . . .
living ruins in a world of living dead!

Temple of Borobudur

Java

The stark, massive grandeur of the Temple of Borobudur (preceding page) in central Java, Indonesia, has stirred the highest aspirations of the Buddhist pilgrims since the ninth century. More than a shrine, the monument was intended to be an embodiment in stone of the doctrines of Mahayana Buddhism. To ascend the terraces of Borobudur is to rise from the base material desires and torments of the flesh, depicted in richly detailed bas-reliefs lining the lower walls, to the spiritual perfection symbolized by the cupola at the summit. The pilgrim is supposed to reach the central and uppermost portion of the temple only after following a long, mandala-shaped (circular) path that winds around each of the diminishing terraces and forms a route that is more than three miles long.

Above left, one of the elaborately decorated main walls of the processional path followed during a pilgrim's journey of gradual enlightenment.

Center, a small, bell-shaped stupa—one of hundreds on Borobudur. The stupa is a hallowed shape in Buddhist doctrine. Believed to derive from pre-Buddhist royal burial mounds, it combines the basic form of the burial mound with that of an umbrella, which is a traditional symbol of rank and authority in the East.

Below left, niches containing statues of the Buddha. In all, there are 463 such vaulted shrines on Borobudur.

Facing page, a small stupa seen from one of the lower terraces, with intricate bas-reliefs on the wall beneath it.

Above left, the upper levels of the temple, culminating in the magnificent central stupa. Seventy-two smaller stupas line the path along these three concentric upper terraces. The latticed openings of the smaller stupas reveal statues of the Buddha within. The intricate bas-reliefs of the previous stages of the ascent have given way to simplicity and openness. The pilgrim has reached the goal of his arduous climb—symbolically, the goal of his entire existence—and has entered the spiritual realm of the Buddhas.

Left, the smaller, openwork stupas, seen from near the summit.

Above right and right, the stone steps that connect the various concentric terraces of Borobudur.

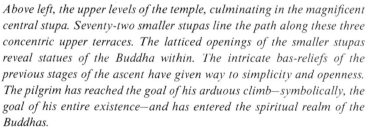

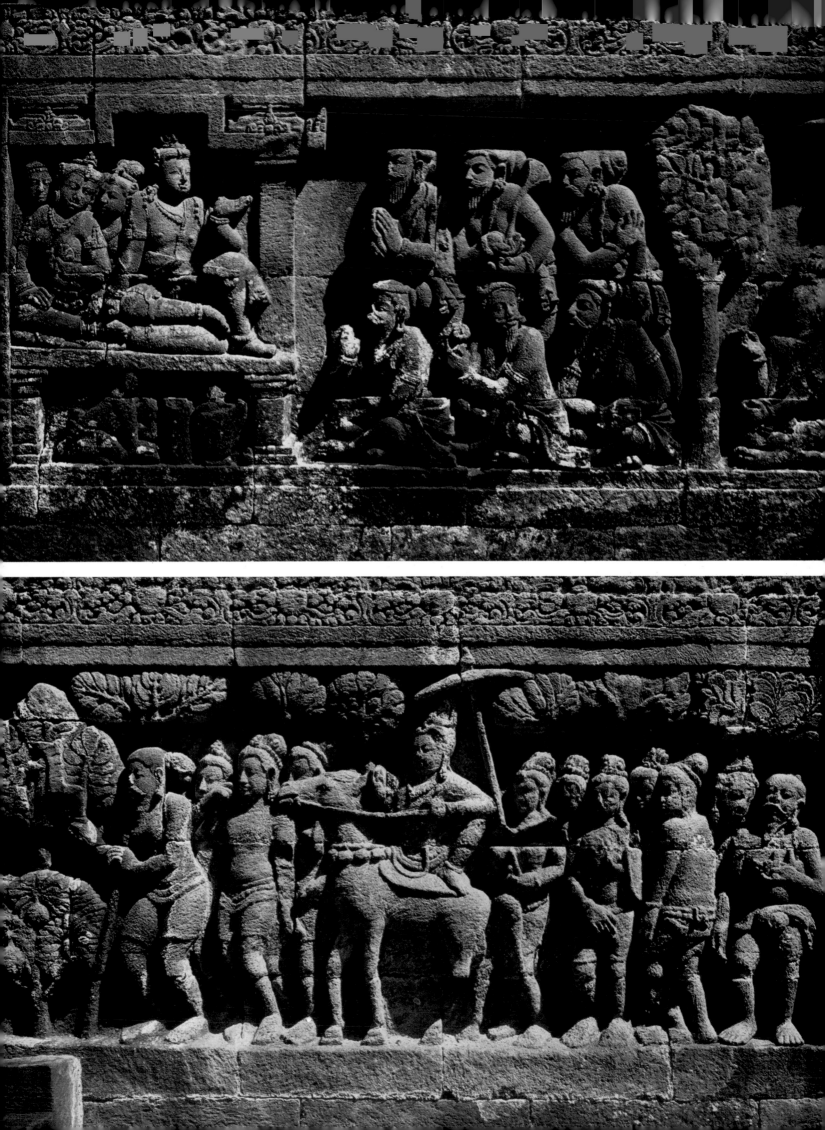

The walls of the four lower galleries of Borobudur are crowded with hundreds of bas-relief panels illustrating Buddhist texts and narratives. The reliefs are approximately three feet high and were intended to be read from right to left. Many of them dramatically depict the imperfections and ceaseless strivings of the unenlightened. Their lively emphasis on human details offers many clues about the courtly rituals and customs of the eighth and ninth centuries.

Left, a group of dignitaries paying their respects to a seated sovereign. Following an Asian custom that persisted into modern times, the sovereign's head is higher than those of his wives. He is sitting on a cushion, which was also a symbol of royalty.

Below left, a relief depicting a procession. The umbrella held above the mounted rider was a perquisite of high rank and royalty.

Right, a relief showing a Harpy (a monster that is half woman, half bird) and a devata, a Buddhist supernatural being.

Although the temple's artists were influenced by Indian Gupta art, the carvings at Borobudur are Javanese in character. This may be partly attributable to the stone used: trachyte, volcanic rock that is common on Java but isn't found anywhere in India. Physical characteristics of the human figures, such as the slanting Oriental eyes, are also distinctly non-Indian.

Facing page, center left, a relief showing the type of vessel that transported Indian traders and colonists to Java. The boat has outriggers as well as a complex system of sails.

Below far right, detail of a relief depicting a king and queen holding court.

Following page, the Buddha Sakyamuni, looking out over the lush, rugged countryside that surrounds the temple.

Temple of Borobudur Java

The pilgrim and the tourist share a common activity—travel—but the psychic gulf that separates them is profound. The tourist who wishes to appreciate the Temple of Borobudur, in central Java, realizes this gulf at once, and he agrees to become, for the moment at least, a pilgrim as well.

Journeying up this symbolic mountain, the visitor is by turns startled, bewildered, and dazed. This is precisely what is meant to happen. Those who built the temple around A.D. 800 had a single purpose in mind: Borobudur was to be a temporal embodiment in stone of the entire spiritual cosmology of Mahayana Buddhism. To climb the steps of the temple is to pass from the lowest plane of existence, repre-

sented by explicit, crowded bas-reliefs that depict carnal torments along the base, to the highest level of spiritual perfection, suggested by the sparse, symbolic constructions at the temple's summit. The path up Borobudur was intended to symbolize the journey toward enlightenment. For the pilgrim who undertakes the journey, the many wonders along the way may ultimately be as significant as the destination itself.

Little is recorded about the origins of Borobudur. It is known that the temple was built during the rule of the Sailendra dynasty (760–860 A.D.), which was largely responsible for introducing Indian religion and architecture into Java. But the building was used as a temple for only a few centuries before it fell into neglect and became overgrown with vegetation. By that time, the Buddhist doctrines the temple glorified were rejected by the Javanese in favor of Islam, and Borobudur was lost to civilization for half a millennium. The temple was discovered in the early nineteenth century by Sir Thomas Stamford Raffles, an official of the British East India Company. Raffles recognized the temple's

significance and initiated the work of clearing away the vegetation, a task that was continued by Dutch archaeologists and not fully completed until 1911. The ruins, so long buried by debris, were initially puzzling. But slowly, as the shape of the temple was gradually revealed, its hundreds of sculptures exposed, and its thousands of bas-reliefs examined, archaeologists were able to glean an understanding of what the original builders had intended when they built the temple.

But the identity of those who built Borobudur remains a mystery. Javanese legend says that the temple was designed by the Indian philosopher Gunadharma and that the humanlike silhouette of the nearby mountain range, which guards the edge of the plain where the temple stands, is a likeness of Gunadharma himself. Whoever the builders were, they were undisputed masters of the complexities of Indian architecture.

The design of Borobudur incorporates three of the most significant symbols found in Indian design—the holy mountain, the mandala, and the stupa. Each of these symbols has its own traditional meaning in Indian thought. By combining

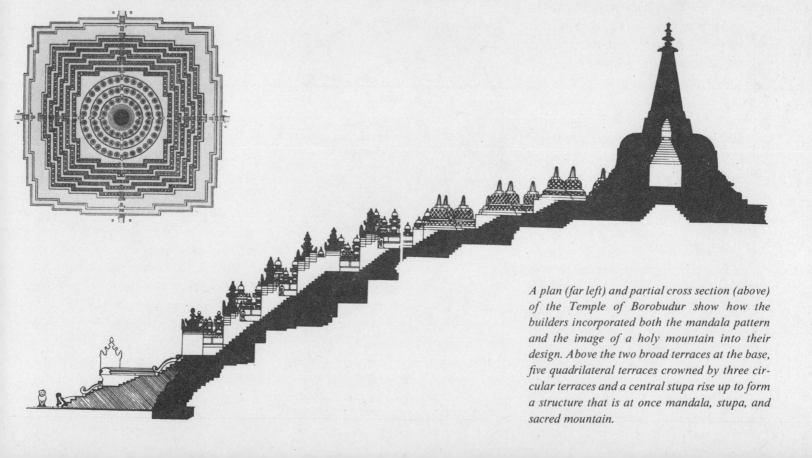

A plan (far left) and partial cross section (above) of the Temple of Borobudur show how the builders incorporated both the mandala pattern and the image of a holy mountain into their design. Above the two broad terraces at the base, five quadrilateral terraces crowned by three circular terraces and a central stupa rise up to form a structure that is at once mandala, stupa, and sacred mountain.

all three symbols into one representational structure, the builders were able to express the subtlety of the Mahayana doctrine in the most comprehensive way possible. Though of differing forms, the holy mountain, mandala, and stupa all convey the same message: the all-embracing nature of the cosmos. An understanding of the meaning of these architectural devices is fundamental to the comprehension of the temple as a whole.

A first glance at Borobudur confirms its mountainlike design. The temple is basically a pyramidal shape on a quadrangular plan. The sides of the base measure over 550 feet, and the stairways in the center of each side ascend to a series of terraces leading to the summit, which is about 127 feet high. Since Borobudur was built on and over a natural hill, it has no interior space. In fact, all of its galleries and terraces are open to the sky.

The concept of the holy mountain originated in Hindu mythology, which maintained that the center of the universe was a golden mountain called Meru, whose foothills were the Himalayas. Meru, the abode of the gods, extended both below and above the earth, thus serving as a symbol of the totality of the cosmos. The people of Java had an additional reason to regard mountains as sacred. The island is dotted with volcanoes, and the periodic destruction wrought by volcanic eruptions was interpreted by the Javanese as being overwhelming evidence of the divine power of mountains. (The volcanoes of Java also provided the material for Borobudur. The temple and all its sculptures and bas-reliefs are constructed entirely from trachyte, a dark-gray volcanic rock common on the island.)

The temple's function as a mandala is most apparent from above. A mandala can assume a pattern of concentric circles (the word *mandala* means "circle" in Sanskrit), rectangles, or even interpenetrating triangles. The mandala is a visual representation of the universe, the macrocosm, which the eye follows from the perimeter to the center along a circuitous path. At Borobudur, it is not the eye and mind alone but the entire body—and, in

Left, engraving from the period of Dutch settlement in Java depicting some European traders. The Dutch first arrived on the island in 1496.

Below, a ninth-century head of what is thought to be either a Buddhist monk or a deified king.

Below left, a medallion showing the Maya-Devi, which is the dream of the Buddha's conception.

theory, the soul—that follow the path. To reach the center of the temple, the visitor is meant to walk around each of the concentric walkways that are encountered on the path upward. Together, they form a route more than three miles long. Each of the four lower walkways is enclosed by a high wall lined with instructive bas-reliefs

and sculptures. In accordance with the belief that it is only possible to "know" one plane of existence at a time, the walls prevent visitors from seeing into, or "knowing," the passageways on other levels. After finding his way to the uppermost rectangular level, the visitor must walk along three additional circular platforms before reaching the main stupa in the center. Thus, the summit of the holy mountain and the center of the mandala are one and the same.

The third symbolic form employed by the builders of Borobudur was the stupa. This is a hemisphere, or half-dome, typically surmounted by a small cone whose symbolic meaning probably originated in pre-Buddhist times when it was used as a burial mound for royalty. At that time, one sign of a king's authority was the umbrella, and the stupa combines the round form of a burial mound with the conical form of a folded umbrella. The stupa became significant to Mahayana Buddhists some time after the death of the Buddha when his corporeal relics were said to have been divided up and interred in various stupas after his death. Eventually, stupas were used to enshrine not only the Buddha's relics but also those of his more notable disciples. If no relics were available, a stupa would be built simply to commemorate an important episode in the Buddha's life. The stupa was the supreme symbol of the Buddha in his transcendent state of immortality.

There are literally hundreds of stupas on Borobudur. The seventy-two on the three uppermost circular terraces are hollowed out and latticed, half revealing the statues of Buddha they enclose. The customary method of paying homage to a stupa is to walk around it, keeping it to the right. The main stupa at the top of the temple is 52 feet in diameter. In addition to the numerous individual stupas, the builders intended the temple as a whole to be regarded as a stupa—a sacred vessel containing the "Eternal Truth of Buddhism." Some Dutch experts who have participated in the restoration of Borobudur suspect that relics of the Buddha were probably buried in the heart of the hill beneath the main stupa. But the relics have yet to be found.

Although many temples in India took the stupa form, Borobudur is usually considered the most elaborate and complex example of the genre. The temple's use of the stupa shape illustrates a paradox that goes to the heart of Mahayana Buddhism: Just as there are many Buddhas and, at the same time, only one Buddha, Borobudur contains many stupas but is itself one enormous stupa—a universe containing many universes.

In accordance with the intricacy of its design, the monument is profusely decorated. The extraordinary bas-reliefs and sculptures along the route to the summit comprise a colorful chronicle of the entire fabric of the Buddhist journey to enlightenment, from the excitement and turmoil

Above, a relief depicting Kertarajasa, ruler of the thriving kingdom of Java in the thirteenth century. Right, bas-relief on the Temple of Borobudur showing a scene from the life of Buddha. Below, an example of a ninth-century Javanese sculpture of a bodhisattva.

of daily life to the repose and serenity of a higher cosmic awareness.

Curiously, the monument's most vivid carvings, which arc along the base, aren't visible. After they were completed, the carvings were covered over with earth fill. Possibly there were fears that the temple might collapse under the weight of the upper structure if the lower walls were not shored up. Or perhaps it was felt that the depiction of the life of the unenlightened was too obvious and detracted from the otherwise ethereal nature of the shrine. It has even been suggested that these "earthy" depictions were somewhat self-consciously and symbolically consigned to the earth. These buried reliefs were discovered in 1885 by J. W. Ijzerman, a Dutch engineer. Some years later, they were cautiously excavated in sections, photographed, and then reburied to protect the foundations.

The 160 buried reliefs depict the *Mahakarmavibhanga*—a text that describes the workings of karmic law, which forms the ethical cornerstone of Buddhism—at the level of *Kamadhatu*, the realm of desire. *Kamadhatu*, the lowest of the three Buddhist planes of existence, corresponds to the natural, material world. According to karmic law, evil deeds are punished by a rebirth fraught with disaster. The artist who executed the now-buried carvings portrayed them with almost unseemly vigor. Hedonists idle their lives away with

Right, an aerial view of the Buddhist Temple of Borobudur. Built around A.D. 800 by the rulers of the Sailendra dynasty, the temple fell into neglect and had become overgrown by about A.D. 1000. It was restored by Dutch archaeologists between 1907 and 1911.

music, dancing, and juggling; and regardless of the temple's intentions, it is rather easy to share these wastrels' enthusiasm. Yet, the scenes are meant to impress the pious pilgrim not only with the consequences of evil but also with the hopeless and eternal circle of earthly desire and torment.

Above the two levels of the foundation are the four rectangular terraces whose walkways are lined with elaborate pinnacles and 463 niches that contain statues of the Buddha, as well as many stupas and bas-reliefs. The terrace reliefs depict tales from numerous sacred texts: from the *Lalitavistara,* which tells how Buddha himself existed in the everyday world; from the *Jatakas,* or birth stories, which are a poetic treatment of many episodes from the Buddha's previous lives on earth; and from the *Gandavyuha,* which tells of Prince Sudhana's journeys from teacher to teacher in search of wisdom. On the fourth gallery, the reliefs recount a tale in which the Maitreya Buddha, or Buddha of the future, is the dominant protagonist.

The lifelike and realistic carvings of the lower galleries, where human figures, elephants, monkeys, and foliage are thickly interwoven, give way to an increasingly stylized form in the upper galleries. The number of human depictions diminishes. In the first gallery, Buddha is still a slave

to the earth and its pleasure, but he sets out on the pathway of salvation by gaining knowledge of poverty, sickness, and death. The second gallery shows him gradually severing his links with passions and worldly temptations. In the third, he has already put the world behind him and is alone with his own consciousness. In the fourth, he has attained *ataraxia*—that perfect capacity for contemplation, a total detachment from the world and from the physical limitations of the body.

Above the fifth terrace, almost at the center of the mandala, stand the three circular terraces, which are devoid of embellishment except for the seventy-two latticed stupas. This is the highest, most enigmatic plane of Buddhist existence, the *Arupadhatu,* or formless world. Here, the world of forms has merged into the world of the void. A well-known Mahayana saying sums it up best: "Form is not different from emptiness; emptiness is not different from form. Form is precisely emptiness; emptiness is precisely form." In the center of the three circular terraces, dominating the whole structure, stands the main stupa. It contains a statue of Buddha that has been left unfinished—hinting, perhaps, that the highest truths can never be fully comprehended. Some authorities believe that this statue was added long after the temple was finished and that the stupa was

originally left empty in deference to the void. Upon reaching the great central stupa, the visitor has completed both his physical and spiritual quest, a quest that ends simultaneously in fulfillment and emptiness.

Temple of the Tooth
at Kandy

Sri Lanka

The Temple of the Tooth (preceding page) in Kandy, Sri Lanka (formerly Ceylon), was begun during the seventeenth century as a shrine for the sacred relic of Buddha's tooth. Additions to the temple have been made almost up to the present day, though most date from the eighteenth and nineteenth centuries. In general, the temple is admired more for the decorative detail of its interior than for its architecture. But its white façade and red roofs are strikingly set off by the green of the surrounding trees and the blue of the artificial lake at Kandy.

Above left, the north side of the temple complex.

Left, a Hindu temple to the god Natha (said to be a bodhisattva, or Buddha-to-be), which stands across the street from the Temple of the Tooth.

Above, the temple complex with its lacy outer wall. The holes in the wall hold lamps on festival days.

Right, a detail of the octagonal corner pavilion which, like the temple as a whole, mingles ancient Buddhist architecture with decorative elements of seventeenth- and eighteenth-century Ceylon. The pavilion now houses a library of palm-leaf manuscripts.

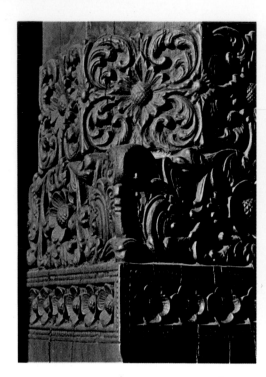

The Temple of the Tooth suffered serious damage during the colonial wars of the late eighteenth century, and as a result, many parts of the temple complex are recent stone reconstructions of the original wooden buildings. Above, an intricately carved wooden column, part of a colonnade adjoining the main temple buildings.

Right, one of the oldest surviving parts of the temple complex. Dating from the seventeenth century, it was built as lodgings for the monks.

Far right, top, the back of the two-story shrine, enclosed within the temple complex, that houses the relic said to be Buddha's tooth. Center, the front of the inner shrine framed by long elephant tusks; the elephant is sacred to Buddha. Bottom, a colonnaded passageway in the front of the temple complex facing the entrance.

Extremely intricate ornamental carving is found throughout the temple complex. Both the capitals and the beams of a long colonnade leading from the main group of temple buildings (left, top and bottom) are covered with sinuous, carved animal forms and rich foliate designs. The pillars and architraves at the rear of the reliquary shrine itself (center) are still more ornate. Although the chief decorative motif is the lotus blossom—Buddhist symbol of the universe—human figures are also depicted on the capitals.

The two-story octagonal pavilion was built by Portuguese captured by the Kandyans during the eighteenth-century colonial wars. The second story of the pavilion is now the library of a Buddhist monastery located on the temple grounds. In midsummer, the pavilion stairs and porch serve as a convenient viewing stand (right) for both resident monks and tourists during the annual festivities of the Esala Perahera pageant in honor of the sacred tooth. At night, deserted and now spectacularly lit by floodlights (below right), the pavilion is reflected in the still water of the canal in front of the temple complex.

In contrast to the rather plain exterior of most of the temple structures, the interiors are often brilliantly decorated. Far left, the entrance to the chapel containing the reliquary. Left, one of the decorative figures on the adjacent wall.

Center left, the second-story of the reliquary temple as seen from the loggia linking it to the external wing of the temple.

Bottom left, exquisitely carved and painted wooden statues in the great hall of a nearby monastery.

Right, two statues of Buddha found in the adjacent monastery. The prone statue recalls, on a smaller scale, the gigantic Reclining Buddha of the temples at Polonnaruva, an ancient capital of Ceylon.

Below, the ornate passageway which leads through the outer temple building to the loggia in front of the reliquary shrine.

Following page, a view from the temple across the manmade lake toward the hilly countryside for which Kandy is known. This terrain is what recommended Kandy as a site for the Sinhalese capital during the seventeenth century, when the lower-lying areas of Ceylon, less easy to defend, were falling to the Portuguese. The lake was created during the nineteenth century by damming and flooding a rice paddy. The rectangular island in the middle was once used to accommodate a king's harem.

Temple of the Tooth at Kandy Sri Lanka

For more than 1,500 years, a miraculously preserved tooth, said to be the Buddha's own, has been a sacred symbol in the life of Sri Lanka—as the island nation formerly called Ceylon has officially been known since 1972. According to ancient Ceylonese legends, the huge tooth was smuggled into the country in A.D. 313 in the hair of an Indian princess who was fleeing a Hindu incursion into her father's kingdom. She had taken the tooth from its Indian shrine because she hoped it would insure her welcome among the Buddhist people of the island. She was not disappointed: The relic quickly became a cult object among the Ceylonese. Over the centuries it was honored in dazzling religious festivals and rituals. Encased in a series of elaborate reliquaries, each one more richly jeweled than the other, it was carried on the backs of elephants in ceremonial processions. More than once, in periods of political unrest, the tooth was stolen, and fabulous stories grew up to explain its habitual return to Ceylon. When succeeding kings established new capitals, they took the tooth with them, and new temples were built to enshrine it.

The present Temple of the Tooth, in Kandy, a city in the center of the country, was begun during the seventeenth century. At this time, the Dutch and Portuguese were fighting for control of Ceylon, and the tooth had become a symbol of a threatened national heritage as well as of a spiritual one. The white wood and stucco temple built to house the tooth seemed as much a monument to the patriotic spirit of the nation as to its Buddhist faith.

The Temple of the Tooth is fronted by a lacelike outer wall, as delicate as filigree, reflected in the calm waters of a canal and a manmade lake. During religious festivals, the wall is lit by the candles inserted into its patterned openings. Above the lake, inside its graceful enclosure, the white walls and red roofs of the temple and the buildings of the King's Palace stand out against the dark green of surrounding tropical vegetation. In the courtyard of the temple complex stands the small, two-story shrine in which the relic is kept.

The temple does not conform to the common Eastern practice whereby each story is smaller than the one below. Indeed, the second floor of the inner shrine actually appears to be wider than the one below because of the verandahs that encircle it. They are used to keep food offerings brought by pilgrims and to store the musical instruments which are sounded to call the priests together for evening prayer.

Below, a nineteenth-century English print of the manmade lake of Kandy, evidently influenced by the Romantic love of the exotic.

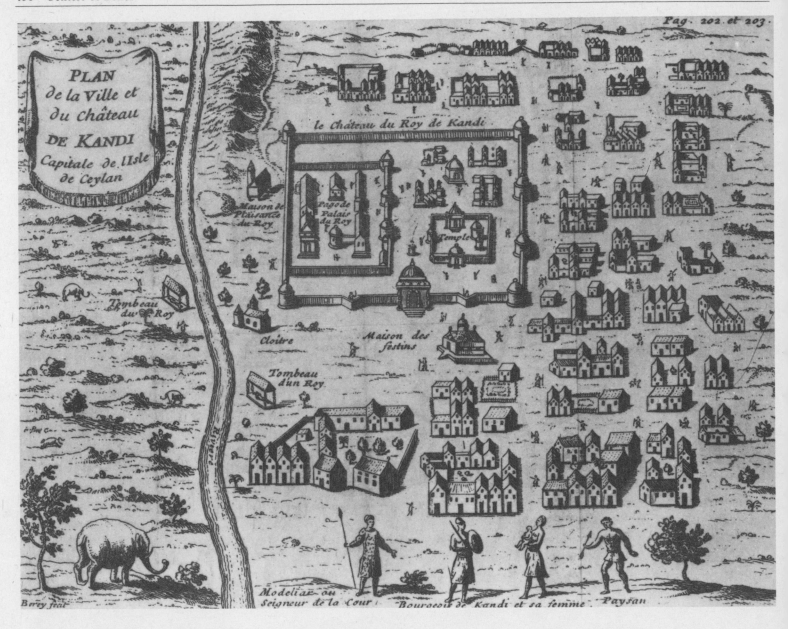

Pag. 202 et 203

PLAN
de la Ville et
du Château
DE KANDI
Capitale de l'Isle
de Ceylan

le Château du Roy de Kandi

Maison de
Plaisance
du Roy

Pagode
Palais
du Roy

Temple

Tombeau
du Roy

Cloître

Maison des
festins

Tombeau
d'un Roy

Modeliar ou
Seigneur de la Cour

Bourgeois de Kandi et sa femme

Paysan

Berey fecit

The sacred tooth is kept in a room on the second floor where it is installed upon a lotus flower of pure gold, within a series of locked jeweled caskets placed upon a low throne. The whole is protected by a cage of gilded iron bars attached to the wall.

The sacred tooth is rarely removed from its customary position, except during the festival known as the Esala Perahera. The celebrations take place at the time of the full moon in late July or early August. For ten days, the streets near the temple are alive with pilgrims and curiosity seekers representing almost every segment of Sri Lankan society. There are barefoot Buddhist monks in saffron robes with brass begging bowls hung around their necks. There are Hindus, descended from the Tamil tribes which settled in northern Sri

Lanka. And there are bronze-skinned Arabs, descendants of early traders, as well as Portuguese, Dutch, and English half-castes—a reminder of the days of European domination. All join in the spectacular annual celebration in which the Sri Lankans symbolically reaffirm their ancient heritage and honor the sacred tooth.

Every night during the Perahera, the tooth relic is removed from its resting place in the temple. Still in its jeweled casket, it is placed on the back of a magnificently adorned elephant flanked by two smaller elephants and borne out of the temple courtyard and into the streets of Kandy. Whip crackers clear the way for the procession of jugglers, torch bearers, drummers, and flutists. Troupes of boy dancers, performing the masculine, acrobatic dances of Ceylon, march along with the descendants of Kandyan aristocrats,

Above, a seventeenth-century French print of the city of Kandy. The Temple of the Tooth probably stood within the walled King's Palace. The "Temple" marked on the map is probably a stupa.

who wear traditional gold shoes, flat gold hats, and heavily brocaded jackets and sashes bearing ceremonial swords. More than a hundred elephants, decked out in gold and brocade, also take part. Among the crowds, Hindu penitents walk on red-hot coals, and at every corner, street vendors offer rice, lotus flowers, and seeds. The pungent odor of camphor and sandalwood is everywhere.

On the last night of the Perahera, the grandest procession of all returns from the city to the Temple of the Tooth. In the darkness, lit only by the candles held by thousands of pilgrims, the outlines of the elephants tower above the crowd. They are led by solemn old men in splendid silk costumes. These elders represent the ancient Sinhalese kings of successive capital cities of the country—Anuradhapura, Polonnaruva, and Kandy—returning to offer the precious relic to their people. For a moment, a great shout drowns out the music, which then picks up again in the incessant rhythms of the dances that follow in the wake of the elephants. Then comes the crowd that flows like a river for miles through the streets of Kandy, until the gold on the doorway of the temple is gleaming in the light of their candles. In an act of worship as old as Buddhism itself, the celebrants move around the pavilion that houses the relic, following the course of the sun. Thousands of voices join in a traditional invocation: "Long life to the Buddha."

Buddhism has held a central position for centuries in Ceylon, and its importance still endures today. A persistent but unsubstantiated legend claims that the founders of the Sinhalese dynasty of Ceylon were closely related to Buddha. This may simply reflect the wholeheartedness with which the Ceylonese later embraced the Buddhist philosophy. It is true that some of the earliest settlers in the country, Indo-Aryan people called the Sinhalas, came from the same northern regions of India as Buddha did. They sailed the Indian Ocean in the sixth century B.C. and discovered an island that seemed an earthly paradise. Its waters were pure, its sky clear, and its climate mild.

To this new land, the Sinhalas brought Brahminic Indian political traditions, a rigid caste system, and their own language—Pali, closely related to Sanskrit—from which developed the present-day language, Sinhalese. Small Sinhalese kingdoms grew up in different parts of the island, but the strongest, at Anuradhapura, in north central Sri Lanka, gradually achieved the most prominence. During the third century B.C., the Indian Emperor Asoka sent his son Mahinda to the island to spread the teachings of Buddha. Mahinda succeeded in converting King Tissa

Right, a plan of the temple. The sacred relic is kept in the shrine in the center of the courtyard indicated by the letters "E" and "F."

Below, a cross section through the two-story shrine that houses the holy relic. Its west door (below right) is decorated with the typical Sinhalese motif of dragons and lotus flowers.

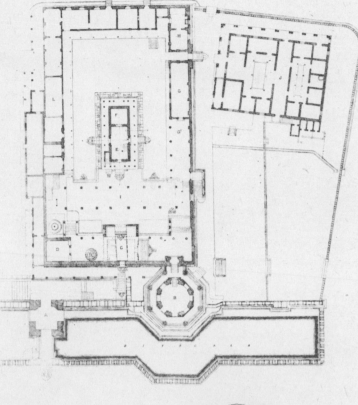

at Anuradhapura, and Tissa's conversion was followed by a rapid spread of Buddhism through all the Sinhalese settlements in the country.

After Tissa's death (ca. 207 B.C.), the island fell into the hands of a tribe from the south of India, the Tamils. A rivalry developed between the Sinhalese and the Tamils that persists in Sri Lanka to this day. The Tamils were Hindus, and so the Buddhism practiced by the Sinhalas came to be as important politically as religiously. Battles between the two peoples

lasted for more than a hundred years, until the reign of a Sinhalese king named Duttagamani, who overthrew the Tamil King Elara. The story is told of how Duttagamani went off to battle with a relic of the Buddha attached to his lance and killed his Tamil rival in single combat. His victory insured the identification of Buddhism with Sinhalese nationalism for centuries to come. Later, in A.D. 313, when the Indian princess stole into the country with Buddha's tooth hidden in her hair, she naturally presented it to the reigning

Sinhalese king. The tooth was placed in a special reliquary temple in the royal park at Anuradhapura and immediately became the national palladium.

During the next seven centuries, the island was ravaged by invasions from the south of India and by internal strife between the Tamils and the Sinhalese. Then, in 1070, a Sinhalese king named Vijaya-bahu shifted the capital—and the sacred tooth—from Anuradhapura to Polonnaruva, a city to the southwest that was easier to defend. The next 150 years was a time of social stability, in many ways the golden age of Ceylon. During this period, the Sinhalese developed considerable expertise in irrigation and water storage, and the huge dams and reservoirs that were constructed greatly enhanced the stature and wealth of the Sinhalese monarchy. Kings were sanctified as bodhisattvas (Buddhas-to-be), and they built many beautiful Buddhist temples in royal parks. The masterpiece among these, in Polonnaruva itself, was the circular Vatadage, built in honor of Buddha's tooth.

Early in the thirteenth century, the Polonnaruva kingdom was weakened by a series of ineffective rulers—a decline from which the Sinhalese did not recover for over three hundred years. At one point, the sacred tooth was abducted by invading soldiers from southern India. During the sixteenth century, the Portuguese, with the

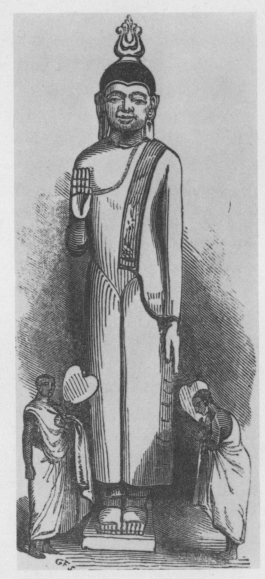

Above, a nineteenth-century engraving depicting a great statue of Buddha before which two priests are meditating.

aim of establishing a profitable trade in Ceylonese ivory and cinnamon, gradually conquered all but the central highlands of Ceylon, which continued to be ruled from Kandy. In 1560, they too carried off the tooth. One story holds that they actually destroyed this heathen idol, first burning it, then pounding it to dust, and casting the ashes to the winds from a ship at sea. But other accounts deny this; and when the Sinhalese established a new capital in Kandy, from which to resist first the Portuguese and later the Dutch, King Vimala Dharma Surya II built a royal temple there for the sacred tooth. Later, his son Narendra Simha—the last king of the Sinhalese line, as it turned out—replaced the crumbling temple with the present Temple of the Tooth. Simha had the relic preserved within the temple in its many jeweled caskets and exhibited it only on rare occasions.

In 1815, the Kandyan kingdom fell—not to the Portuguese nor to the Dutch, but to the British who had seized the Dutch lowland colonies at the beginning of the Napoleonic Wars. In the decades that followed, Ceylonese society and government were in many ways irrevocably changed. Today, Sri Lanka is a sovereign member of the British Commonwealth, with a parliamentary government. Even so, every year the ministers of the government make a point of traveling to Kandy from the present-day capital of Colombo to dedicate themselves to their public office before the shrine in the courtyard of the temple. And thousands of pilgrims journey to Kandy every summer to take part in the Esala Perahera. Whether Buddha's tooth is actually there or not, the pride and history of a nation are indisputably enshrined in the Temple of the Tooth.

Left, an ancient stone carving from the entrance pavilion of the temple.

Mostar

Yugoslavia

Preceding page, the great bridge over the Neretva River, symbol of Mostar and its best-known landmark. Known as the Stari Most, or Old Bridge, it was designed by the Turkish architect Hajrudin and completed in 1566.

Left and above, the slender minaret of the most beautiful mosque in Mostar—the Karadžozbeg Mosque, the "mosque of the black-eyed bey." (A bey was a provincial governor in the Ottoman Empire.) The building, built in 1557, has a large central dome above a square base and three smaller domes over its portico (facing page). The madrasa, or religious school, adjoining the mosque is still a center of Islamic learning.

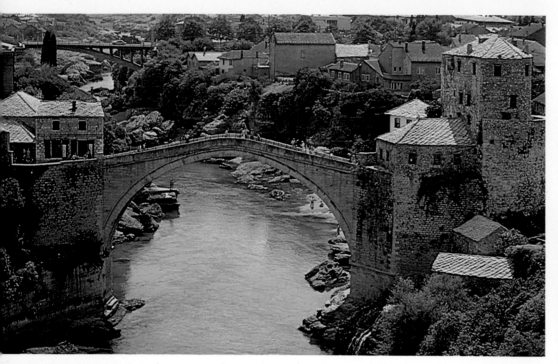

Top and near right, the Old Bridge, showing the fortified towers that guard the passageway. Constructed in 1676, the tower, called Tara, on the left bank, was probably used for storing ammunition. Halebija Tower, on the right bank, is unusually tall and served as both prison and guardhouse.

Above and far right, the Kujundžiluk, the ancient quarter of Mostar near the bridge. Tiled roofs, shuttered windows, and bright colors reveal the Slavic, Turkish, and Italian influences on these sixteenth- and seventeenth-century buildings.

The Karadžozbeg Mosque incorporates ornamentation typical of the Ottoman style. Built by a wealthy landowner said to be a native of nearby Potok, it is the most important Islamic monument in the city. Several other mosques and shrines built in the sixteenth and seventeenth centuries also helped establish Mostar as a religious center. The madrasa, completed in 1570, drew numerous Islamic scholars to Mostar. Many of the city's most impressive monuments, including the Karadžozbeg Mosque and the Old Bridge, were constructed within the span of a single decade, from 1556 to 1566.

The spacious arcade leading to the door of the mosque (right and below near right) is covered with three small domes, a design characteristic of Turkish architecture during the sixteenth century. In the background is a fountain for ritual washing, surrounded by white columns supporting an arcade.

The geometric construction of the Karadžozbeg Mosque, based on a combination of circular domes on polygonal bases, allows a maximum amount of open space within the building. The Islamic love of geometric ornamentation is evident in the decorations above the door (below far right).

The interior of the Karadžozbeg Mosque, with its graceful yet monumental Ottoman style, reveals the influence on Turkish architects of the Byzantine church of Hagia Sophia. The architect of the mosque is unknown.

Above, the mihrab, a recess in the wall that faces toward Mecca, vaulted with a crystalline half dome. The circular window panes contain colored glass from Murano outside Venice, denoting the influence of Dalmatia and Italy. Bright floral designs found throughout the mosque (below right) are typically Turkish.

Following page, the dome and minaret of the Mosque of Koski Mehmed Pasha. This mosque, built in 1618, has painted interior decorations that are over three hundred years old.

Mostar Yugoslavia

Nestled among green mountains, on the banks of the Neretva River, lies the delightful little town of Mostar. With its colorful red roofs and old white stone houses and its graceful arched bridge, the town is at first glance reminiscent of villages in Provence or Tuscany. But almost immediately, the skyline of Mostar reminds the visitor that he is indeed in the capital of Herzegovina, a region in Yugoslavia. Mosques and their minarets dot the city, and many old Turkish houses and baths remain as evidence of the long period of Ottoman domination.

The Turks were not the only invaders to occupy the town. The history of this region of Yugoslavia is a history of many wars and occupations. Indeed, the earliest written records about the region come from the Romans, who called the area Illyri-cum. They refer to a town named Cim, renowned for its good wine, and to another called Andretium—a name which at one time signified the capital of a Roman province and, therefore, a town of some prominence. It is unlikely, however, that either of these stood on the site of present-day Mostar, and Roman ruins are common throughout the region.

Today, wars seem far away, and Mostar is characterized by a quiet peace. Tourists come to admire its Turkish architecture—in particular the Karadžozbeg Mosque and the famous bridge which is the true heart of the town. The bridge is known in Serbo-Croatian as Stari Most, or Old Bridge. The city is traditionally thought to be named after it, although, in fact, the name Mostar was first recorded over a hundred years before the bridge was built. Another theory suggests that Mostar means "keeper of the bridge." In any case, the bridge became a celebrated landmark soon after its completion, and has become the symbol of the town.

The Ottoman occupation of the region, under which Mostar was to become, for many years, the center of Islamic thought, dates back to the end of the fourteenth century. On the morning of June 15, 1389, the Serbian army faced the Turks on the gently rolling fields of Kosovo, among the mountains that separate Serbia from Macedonia. The Serbian force, bolstered by troops from Bosnia, Wallachia, and other Slavic states, was no longer as strong as it had been under the great Serbian ruler Stephen Dushan. Half a century earlier, Dushan had forged a Slavic kingdom stretching from the Adriatic to the Aegean and from the Danube to the Gulf of Corinth. In the ensuing years, however, rivalry between feudal barons as well as civil and religious strife had weakened royal authority and power. Even so, the Serbian army was still the only power in the Balkans capable of stopping the Turks on their westward march. The army was headed by Lazar, who is said to have refused the title of czar used by his predecessors and was known by the more modest title of Prince of Serbia.

The Turks, led by the Ottoman Sultan Murad I, were confident of success. For almost a century and a half, the Turkish army had been undermining what remained of the once glorious Byzantine Empire. From the steppes of Turkestan the Turks had gradually moved across the Caucasus and through Asia Minor. After their success at Adrianople, the last outpost of Byzantium, they had only to press westward past the Serbian barrier to gain

Left, an engraving depicting typical Turkish dwellings of the time when the Ottomans ruled Mostar. When the Turkish ruler of Herzegovina established his headquarters in the town, Mostar grew from a garrison into a regional center of culture and trade.

control of the entire Balkan Peninsula. Militarily confident and fervently religious, they could depend on the wide experience of the *spahis,* lightly armed but highly mobile cavalry, and the feared *janissaries,* young Christians who had been converted to Islam and drafted into the army. Utmost discipline and rigorous training had molded them into an exceptionally fierce and dependable regiment.

At the end of that decisive day in 1389, the Slavic army had been routed, and the Turks were free to push farther on toward the Danube. In spite of the victory, the last Serbian fortress did not fall until 1459, six years after Constantinople itself had finally been conquered. By the end of the century, Bosnia, Herzegovina, Montenegro, and Bulgaria had all been absorbed by the Ottoman Empire, and Turkish forces were a potential threat to Budapest and Vienna.

While the westward and northward conquest continued, the new regime began to consolidate its holdings in the Balkans. Little Mostar, first mentioned as a settlement in 1440, became a strategically crucial area since it controlled the road that stretched from the large and important city of Sarajevo to Ragusa, the rich Latin maritime republic on the Adriatic. The Turks left Ragusa untouched, so that it might serve as trading center and point of contact with unconquered lands. In addition, Mostar held a key position for the control of the whole Neretva River valley, and the Turks were quick to establish a strong garrison there once they had conquered the region.

Mostar's military significance brought it a new political prominence, and in 1522 the Turkish governor of the area established his headquarters there. Increasing numbers of soldiers, merchants, and administrators settled in Mostar, and the town grew and prospered. With this new expansion came civic improvements and embellishments. And in 1566, after nine years of work, Mostar completed the Old Bridge, which was constructed to replace a primitive suspension span that had hung from chains over the Neretva River.

More than one critic, impressed by the splendid simplicity of the bridge, has described it as a masterpiece of Turkish secular art. An unadorned arch of a white stone known locally as *tenelija,* the Old Bridge has a span of almost one hundred feet and stands sixty-five feet above the river. Hump-backed and cobbled, it is fortified at both ends by imposing towers,

supported by massive abutments which were erected in the seventeenth century. The contrasting heaviness of these structures accentuates the overall grace of the design.

The man responsible for this remarkable achievement was a Turkish architect named Hajrudin, a disciple of the brilliant Koji Sinan. Sinan, a contemporary of Michelangelo and one of the most original Ottoman architects, built a masterpiece of his own—the bridge over the Drina near Gorazde, also in Herzegovina—only five years after the Old Bridge at Mostar was completed. He is better known as the chief theorist and master of the geometric style characteristic of Ottoman building, which placed round domes on top of square spaces to create spacious interiors suggestive of those of Western architecture.

Sinan's ideas are also seen in the design of Mostar's other architectural triumph.

Above left, the Herceguša Tower, which dates from the fifteenth century. This tower is all that remains of the fortifications that originally protected Mostar from the Turks.

Above and left, Mostar street scenes, depicting the Turkish influence which lingered well into the twentieth century.

The different religions and customs of Herzegovina make local graveyards particularly interesting. Left, a typical pillar in Mostar's Moslem cemetery. Right, narrative scenes on a tombstone in nearby Bosnia.

Left, a Turkish tombstone in Bosnia, elaborately decorated with a geometric pattern based on floral motifs. Such patterns are typical of Ottoman art and are frequently found on mosques and other Turkish buildings.

Around the same time that the Old Bridge was being constructed, work was finished on the most beautiful mosque in the city, the Karadžozbeg Džamija, or "mosque of the black-eyed bey." (A bey is a Turkish title of honor, signifying a governor, prince, or lord.)

The Karadžozbeg Mosque is an elegant domed building laid out on typically Ottoman lines—not particularly large, but unusually harmonious in design. A portico, which contains a fountain for ritual washing, leads to the interior. There the *mihrab,* a niche in the wall facing Mecca, is covered with a delicate crystalline vault. The mosque's huge dome is accented on the exterior by an exceptionally slender minaret, made of the same white stone as the Old Bridge, and by three smaller cupolas above the porch. The solid walls look as if they were made of one single block, for the Turks were skillful builders. It is said that thousands of eggs were mixed with the mortar they used. The round glass windows are made of red, brown, blue, and white glass from Murano, an island suburb of Venice famous for its glassware.

Completing the mosque is an adjoining *madrasa,* or religious school. This brought many serious Islamic scholars to Mostar and signaled the beginning of a period of intense growth in the town.

During the early seventeenth century, the citizens of Mostar built several more mosques and opened numerous bazaars. Mostar soon became a center for craftsmen of every sort, especially tanners, tailors, and goldsmiths, who formed guilds and gathered in prescribed areas to sell their wares. On the left bank of the Neretva, for example, near the Old Bridge is the Kujundžiluk, the quarter where the goldsmiths had their heavily shuttered shops. Today this quarter still affords a glimpse into a very different past.

Mostar grew culturally and intellectually as it prospered economically. Its warm and sunny climate—its temperatures are often the highest in Europe during the midsummer months—coupled with the attractive surroundings, drew poets, writers,

and thinkers from throughout the Balkans. It became one of the chief cultural centers of the Slavic "renaissance" and was affectionately referred to as the "cradle of poets," the "mother of wisdom and poetry," and the "gateway to the warm sea."

Politically, Mostar was a center of Pan-Slavism—a movement for Slavic unity and independence—that often provided the citizens of Mostar with opportunities to show the courage and determination which are such an integral part of the Slavic character. Today, the courage of Mostar's youth is exhibited again each June in a spectacle that brings citizens and tourists together along the banks of the Neretva under the Old Bridge. Above them, among the streamers and banners that deck the bridge, the young men of the town prepare to dive into the water sixty-five feet below. Some simply plunge down; others try more elaborate and spectacular feats. The attempt alone is an act of bravery—or bravado.

Like most of the Balkans, Mostar remained under Ottoman rule—albeit resentfully—until well into the nineteenth century. In 1878, however, the Austro-Hungarian army arrived at the city on a mission of "liberation." This mission was not welcomed by many of the inhabitants. Although they had no chance of any military victory against the well-trained imperial troops of the Hapsburgs, the rebels reaffirmed Mostar's position as the ideological center of the Slavs.

The Hapsburg occupation brought with it an excellent administration, an efficient civil service, and the cultural and economic ideas of Western Europe. And the small capital of Mostar once again became a flourishing intellectual center. The heroes of the patriotic movement—Aleksa Šantić, Svetozar Ćorović, Javan Dučič, Osman Đikič, and others—were also literary heroes who ran a local nationalistic journal. They are remembered today both in streets of the city which are named after them and in such events as the "poetic evenings of Šantić," which are a celebrated literary tradition.

For many of the town's inhabitants, the most revered monument in Mostar is no longer the Old Bridge or the Karadžozbeg Mosque, but the partisan cemetery on a hill overlooking the city. This peaceful spot, with its green terraces and curved white walls, is a lovely commemoration of the sacrifice of the citizens of Mostar who fought against the fascists during World War II. And from the hillside there is a panoramic view over Mostar, including the slender bridge, the round domes of the mosques and their graceful minarets, and

Above, view from the Neretva River showing the graceful minarets and rounded domes which dominate the skyline of the city. Many of these buildings were erected during the early years of Ottoman rule, the period of Mostar's greatest expansion.

the gray stone and red roofs of the old quarter.

Yugoslavia, for so long the site of wars and political upheaval, is now a peaceful and thriving nation. The town of Mostar provides a picturesque link with the past, with the traditions and heritage of the Slavic people.